Celtic Folk Magic Traditions

Ancient Practices, Nature Wisdom, and Sacred Traditions Rooted in Celtic Heritage

Brigid Rowan

Celtic Folk Magic Traditions

Ancient Practices, Nature Wisdom, and Sacred Traditions Rooted in Celtic Heritage

Brigid Rowan

Table of Contents

Introduction 1

Chapter 1: A Living Thread: What Makes Celtic Folk Magic Folk 5

Chapter 2: Peoples and Times: Historical Roots and Regional Frames 20

Chapter 3: Speaking with the Land: Place, Spirit, and Reciprocity 36

Chapter 4: The Turning Year: Seasonal Rhythms and Folk Calendars 52

Chapter 5: Plants as Teachers: Trees, Herbs, and Hedgerow Wisdom 68

Chapter 6: Stones, Water, and Weather: Elemental Kinships 84

Chapter 7: Hearth and Threshold: Household Protections and Blessings 99

Chapter 8: Tokens, Threads, and Tools: Objects with Story 115

Chapter 9: Boundaries and Belonging: Ethics for the Curious 131

Chapter 10: Carrying the Flame: A Thoughtful Path Forward 148

Conclusion 163

Reference List 167

Introduction

On a dusky evening, you might find yourself pausing as your grandmother gently ties a red thread around your wrist, her hands steady and warm. Or maybe you've stood beside neighbors at a quiet well, each of you leaving a ribbon or whispering a wish into the cool air. For some, these moments are family memory; for others, they're half-remembered stories or a longing stirring beneath everyday life. These acts aren't about spectacle—they live in fleeting gestures, shared bread, a word spoken to the land, the simplest kindness offered at a threshold. Right here, in the ordinary magic of tea shared at dawn or footsteps tracing old paths, we find the living heart of Celtic folk customs.

But how does anyone truly connect to ancestral traditions in our busy, modern lives? Where do you begin if you want to honor nature, spirit, or place without resorting to imitation or stepping where you shouldn't? What's the difference between participating in a vibrant tradition and accidentally crossing into appropriation—or losing yourself in an avalanche of social media "how-tos" and one-size-fits-all rituals? Maybe you're searching for belonging that feels safe and genuine. Perhaps you wonder if it's possible to be both curious and respectful, creative and careful, as you explore practices tangled up with history, pain, and resilience.

Introduction

This book is here to help you answer those questions—not by handing you strict formulas, but by meeting you where you are: curious, caring, and perhaps a bit overwhelmed. Together, we'll uncover what makes Celtic folk magic unique—a tapestry woven from daily acts of care and relationship, not distant, mysterious spells. Here, you'll find clear historical context, practical ways to reflect, and guidance to walk with confidence and humility. Instead of promising easy answers, I'll offer you the tools to trace your own path, nurturing connection to your heritage, to the natural world, and to your own sense of meaning.

I know that stepping into these traditions can feel risky. There's pressure to 'get it right,' anxiety about causing harm, and endless advice—sometimes contradictory—on what's allowed or authentic. Many readers worry about being outsiders, misusing what isn't theirs, or losing touch with their values in pursuit of something meaningful. You might carry questions about gender, sexuality, inclusion, or safety; maybe you're looking for community that welcomes every part of who you are. If you feel lost among gatekeepers and trend-chasers, take heart: this space centers your journey, embracing both uncertainty and hope.

For years, my work has been rooted in Celtic landscapes—listening to local storytellers, sharing meals with families who still bless their doorways and wells, unraveling histories buried in archives and remembered in song. As a cultural historian and folklorist, my writing brings together research, lived experience, and lessons learned firsthand from those who keep these ways alive. My commitment is always to ethical engagement: honoring sources, asking permission, and holding space for voices often left out. With this in mind, I invite you not as a distant expert but as a guide walking beside you—ready to share, learn, and listen.

You'll notice that the chapters flow like a winding stream, each one building on the last. We'll start by exploring why everyday actions—like sweeping the hearth or tying a simple knot—carry such enduring power. Then, we'll travel through the rich history of Celtic-speaking peoples, discover how landscape shapes tradition, and learn to read the turning year through festivals, weather, and memory. Later chapters will reveal the wisdom of plants and stones, the care woven into household protections, the meaning behind charms and sacred objects, and the ethics of practicing in today's diverse, interconnected world. Finally, we'll glimpse how you might carry these threads forward—with authenticity, accountability, and joy.

What sets this book apart is its devotion to complexity, context, and care. Full stories are given breath here, not just fragments. Regional distinctions matter—Irish, Scottish, Welsh, Breton, and beyond—so no voice is erased for convenience. You'll find trauma-informed perspectives that honor living communities and hard histories. There is no dogma, no appropriation, and no demand for purity or perfection. Instead, this work foregrounds inclusion, honors LGBTQ+ and marginalized voices, and puts environmental stewardship at the core of spiritual practice. If you value authenticity and compassion over performance or exclusivity, you are welcome here.

Introduction

You're invited to treat this book as a companion on an ongoing journey—not as an instruction manual, but as a space for reflection and discovery. Throughout, you'll encounter journaling prompts, exercises in observation, and invitations to ask better questions. You are free to move slowly, to adapt ideas gently, and to return again and again with fresh eyes. These pages offer a way to belong without needing a flawless pedigree or special initiation—just curiosity, respect, and openness to learning. Your story, identity, and intuition all have a place in this living tradition.

So, let's step in together—with open hands and humble hearts. Bring your doubts, your excitement, your longing to reconnect. Within these chapters, you'll find stories, guidance, and encouragement to deepen your bond with heritage, land, and self. The first chapter awaits, ready to show you how the simplest acts—a thank-you whispered at a well, a blessing said with each sweep of the floor—can open doors to enchantment found in ordinary days. Welcome to the adventure. Let's begin.

Chapter 1: A Living Thread: What Makes Celtic Folk Magic Folk

Imagine two neighbors each putting a small amount aside every week. One puts it all into a single, well-known savings account while the other spreads their money across several different options—some safe, some a bit uncertain. As months pass, their total savings grow in very different ways, shaped by choices that respond to daily life needs and risks. This example isn't about finance but about how simple actions, made consistently over time and shaped by local knowledge and experience, weave into something bigger and lasting.

Just like these investment strategies affect financial outcomes, so too do the everyday acts and beliefs in Celtic folk magic influence its ongoing life and meaning. In this chapter, we'll explore how the ordinary, practical gestures rooted in community and tradition form a living thread, holding the past and present together. We'll look at what truly makes these practices 'folk' by considering how shared experience, place, and relationship shape the way Celtic magic is done and passed on—not through grand ceremonies but through humble acts woven into daily rhythms.

Chapter 1: A Living Thread: What Makes Celtic Folk Magic Folk

Everyday Enchantment Defined

Magic rarely looks like it does in stories, with waving wands and grand proclamations. In Celtic folk traditions, magic slips quietly into the corners of ordinary life. A pinch of salt at the door, water sprinkled over a sleeping child, a whispered thanks to a tree—these are acts shaped by daily needs, not by spectacle. Magic dwells in what is useful, familiar, and close at hand.

Many readers come to this subject wondering how everyday enchantment passes from one generation to the next. We'll explore how these stories traveled in the next section, but first, let's settle in with what makes an act or belief truly "folk." Folk practice means knowledge held by people together—woven through households, neighborhoods, and work. Its authority does not depend on formal titles or sacred texts. Instead, trust grows as neighbors recall what their elders did before them: "my grandmother always…" or "that's how we do it here." The acts themselves are shaped by local need and memory. Someone may sprinkle salt across the threshold to shield against ill luck, while a temple ceremony might use incense consecrated through careful ritual. Both intend blessing, but only one roots itself in the kitchen, at dawn, beside a burning fire. Folk magic happens within the rhythm of tending cattle, turning bread, cleaning floors. Gesture joins with task, so prayer becomes part of sweeping, spinning, baking, or sowing.

Formal religions often set apart their rituals—special days, sacred places, trained leaders. Folk religion, by contrast, lives in the spaces in between: liminal times like sunrise and threshold places like doors or crossroads. Its wisdom answers the questions that press closest. Redfield explained this difference as a meeting of two currents—a great tradition handed down in books and led by scholars, and a little tradition carried by villagers who learned by watching and doing (Burnett, 2000). These bands are never fully separate. Even when world religions introduce new prayers or objects, everyday folkways adapt those tools for their own purposes. Sacred texts might join old customs, reimagined for local use. When misfortune comes, some blame fate or past actions, following the higher tradition, but many turn to views shaped by folk beliefs—perhaps suspecting a jealous neighbor or a wandering spirit instead (Burnett, 2000).

Relationship sits at the heart of folk magic. Reciprocity—the mutual care and respect given in return for gifts—is its ethical core. Offerings at wells, a word to the land, or food left for unseen guests all acknowledge relationship rather than demand payment. Power comes from right relationship, not control. Just as you thank a neighbor for help, you might nod to the apple tree that shades your home. Nature becomes participant; the wind, rain, stones, and streams respond to words and gestures, bearing witness or carrying wishes. Later chapters will show these relationships in action at wells and hearths; for now, notice the principle: enchantment grows in courtesy and attention, not secrecy and domination.

Celtic folkways bear the mark of place. Geography breathes form into custom. A coastal household might sweep sand out the back door on a waxing tide for luck. Upland villages work wool charms, read clouds for omens, or use stone beside the hearth for protection. To bless a child, one parish ties red thread, another sets iron by the cradle, another hangs hawthorn above the lintel. No universal handbook exists; transmission relies on memory, voice, and close observation. What holds true in one valley can be unknown just over the ridge. This diversity gives the tradition its flavor and strength. Oral pathways—how these songs, gestures, and recipes move from hand to hand—are the focus of the next section.

Folk practices rarely stand still. Thresholds, first fruits, sunwise circles—these patterns endure even as ingredients change. When iron nails become scarce, a steel pin steps in, yet the protective intention lives on. Social pressures shift customs too. New laws, church teachings, or economic changes reshape where and when old acts continue. Still, communities narrate each adjustment: "we do it this way now because…" The story carries the thread, keeping continuity alive amid change. Later chapters will offer both the historical context for these shifts and guidance for adapting practices today with care and respect.

For readers concerned about making mistakes or overstepping, consider this: folk magic asks relationship, awareness, and humility—not perfection. To honor living tradition is not to copy but to listen, to take part with gratitude. Recognizing the force of local habit, memory, and relationship is the ground upon which respectful engagement stands.

Lineages of Story and Practice

Everyday enchantment thrives in what people do at home, on the land, and among their neighbors—worn stories, handed-down gestures, and crafts repeated by many hands. Understanding what makes practices folk raises an immediate question: how did these everyday customs persist and travel across generations without priests, books, or formal schools? The answer begins with the living web of oral transmission, family ties, and connection to place, all working together to anchor Celtic folk magic as something shared, remembered, and remade in daily life.

Oral traditions form the backbone of communal memory. In times and places where few could read, stories, proverbs, riddles, and songs carried practical wisdom alongside entertainment. For example, a tale about greeting a hollow might encode how to safely approach unfamiliar landforms, while a proverb like "Never turn your back at a meeting of roads" preserves both social etiquette and navigation smarts. These oral forms were crafted to stick—they use rhythm, rhyme, repetition, and sometimes a twist or lesson that makes them easy to recall even in stressful moments or while working. Far from being childish or mystical, they acted as mnemonic tools, making sure guidance was both portable and hard to forget (UNESCO, 2019).

Recitation, singing, and storytelling happened at home, during chores, or at seasonal gatherings. Such performances weren't limited to any one group; children, parents, and elders all listened and participated, shaped by context and audience. Some expressions belonged to everyone—a harvest rhyme or communal blessing—while others were reserved for those recognized for their skill or standing. Across much of Europe, local storytellers and poets were treasured as keepers of collective memory. In Gaelic Ireland and Scotland, seanchaí and bards played this role, while in Wales, cyfarwyddiaid served in similar ways. Storytelling wasn't always public performance; it often took the quiet form of a bedside tale or an urgent warning during a walk through high grass.

With oral knowledge, meaning often shifted slightly in each telling. Context mattered—who told the story, who listened, and where it happened changed its details. Because these traditions were fragile, their survival depended on an unbroken chain: one generation passing words and habits directly to the next (UNESCO, 2019). This made everyday settings—the kitchen by the hearth, a path by the field, a gathering after supper—central classrooms for folk magic. Customary acts lived in song and story, and language itself was a vessel for keeping enchanted ways alive.

Within the household, authority flowed from demonstrated care and skill rather than official titles. Grandmothers, midwives, and craftworkers held trusted positions because of steady hands and wise hearts. Their right to teach sprang from community trust and lived experience, not ceremonies or written credentials. New learners joined in by watching, helping, and copying, not by sitting through lessons. A grandchild watched a knot tied against bad dreams, memorizing steps not through explanation but through the practiced movement of familiar hands. During childbirth, a young helper absorbed midwifery customs by holding cloths or preparing herbs, learning not only what to do but also when and why. Handmade objects—charmed stitches in clothing, carved butter patterns, plaited rushes—carried lessons inside them. Their shapes, timing, materials, and intention mirrored what the maker knew and valued. People understood that homemade charms held more weight than items bought from strangers, because embedded knowledge gave them power.

Place shaped learning as much as lineage did. Certain wells, fields, cliffs, and shorelines became living classrooms where custom taught itself. Community members picked up rituals, weather lore, or protective gestures by returning to such sites again and again. Paths trodden daily, or pilgrimages taken yearly, created regular opportunities for repeating and reinforcing tradition. Hazards and gifts found in each region shaped what and how people learned; coastal folk might master sea-blessing rituals and shellcraft, while those inland kept stone and weather lore close at hand. Authenticity here meant practice that fit the ground—customs adapted to the quirks and risks of real places, not generic routines borrowed from far away. If a rite matched the needs of its people and land, it could be trusted as rooted and meaningful.

Memory aids helped bridge gaps between knowing, acting, and remembering. Verses guided hands and feet, marking steps for tying spells or counting stitches: each word lined up with motion, so nothing got skipped during tense moments. Knots, spirals, patterned weavings, and small charms held structure for both thought and body, cueing not just what to do but how to feel and focus. Tokens tucked into pockets—an old coin, a blessed pin, a sprig of rowan—stood as reminders of wider instructions or tales heard at bedtime. These things were not magical in themselves. Their strength came from sparking memory and linking the present act to the wider web of shared story and intent (UNESCO, 2019).

Transmission flourished in communities open to adaptation, shaped by broader webs of kinship, labor, and festival that will appear more clearly in later chapters. While some lines broke or changed under pressure—migration, religious change, or colonization—the pathways remain visible in stories, customs, and cherished objects. Folk magic's roots thrive in plurality: no single pathway carries all truth, and authentic practice means listening for grounded resonance rather than chasing purity. With these pathways in view, readers can now set careful boundaries for inquiry and approach these traditions with mindful respect and humility.

Scope of This Study

Now that we've seen how these practices traveled through generations—through storytelling, household routines, and local landscape—the focus now turns to the kind of exploration this book offers. Rather than guiding you through spells or step-by-step instructions, these pages invite contemplation instead of replication. They offer a view into the cultural expressions woven into everyday acts: blessing a threshold, tending a well, sharing bread with neighbors. The intent is for readers to recognize recurring patterns like attention to edges and seasons, rather than treating these customs as formulas. This book doesn't promise results or personal power. Instead, it helps you see how gestures and beliefs reflected community understanding of reciprocity, safety, and belonging (Ó Giolláin, 2000). As you read, you'll gain skills in noticing motifs—a red thread here, a water offering there—without feeling called to perform them as if chasing authenticity.

Expectations for what's ahead are clear from the beginning. This is a cultural-historical exploration. You'll encounter living customs and stories linked not only to spiritual worlds but also to farming cycles, daily survival, and neighborhood bonds. At every turn, the hope is to equip you to engage curiously and respectfully. Folk magic in this context isn't a system waiting to be reconstructed; it's a living thread tied to real places and people. Every tradition described links back to a locale and its speakers. Rather than presenting techniques to take on as your own, the study invites you to listen in—learning about the custom as much as the spirit behind it (Dorson, 1972). Patterns may echo across borders, but each retains its own voice and rhythm.

The examples chosen throughout draw mainly from Irish, Scottish, Welsh, and Breton contexts. This regional awareness will help you understand why a rowan twig hanging over a Highland door and a Welsh threshold charm both address protection, yet their meanings, timing, and associated stories differ. Whenever possible, language and place are identified: "In Munster," "From the Outer Hebrides," "A Cornish custom." Descriptions highlight similarities—like shared motifs of water, wells, or knots—while drawing out distinctions that matter within each tradition. When comparable practices are presented together, it's not because they are identical, but to reveal how communities shaped their own responses to landscape, climate, church influence, or neighboring cultures (Evans-Wentz, 1911). In later chapters, you'll encounter how the history and terrain of each region colored practices—whether it's the survival of ancient holy wells in Ireland, mountain boundary customs in Scotland, or hearth blessings in Brittany.

It's tempting to look for a single "Celtic" system, especially when parallels jump out—a belief in fairy folk here, a healing ritual there. Yet, shared features often reflect rural lifeways, agricultural rhythms, or waves of Christianization, not an ancient unified religion. A word or name in one tradition may carry very different weight elsewhere. For example, the Irish aos sí, Scottish sìth, and Welsh Tylwyth Teg each evoke fairy-like presences, but their roles, appearances, and stories mirror their own landscapes and histories. Assuming they are interchangeable flattens the nuances of their communities. The regional diversity found here arose from migrations, colonizing pressures, and shifting religious influences across centuries (MacNeill, 1959). Careful attention to terminology and origin helps keep alive the unique character of each strand within this living weave.

Responsible curiosity runs throughout these pages. Readers are invited to question where a story or practice comes from—whether it's a fieldworker's notebook, family memory, Victorian antiquarian collection, or modern retelling. Every version carries traces of the time, collector, and motives behind its recording: sometimes a wish to celebrate, sometimes nostalgia, sometimes even commercial agendas. When tales don't fully align from place to place, the intent here is to hold plurality rather than forcing a "correct" account. Folk traditions shift and adapt, sometimes wildly. Asking "Who told this, when, and why?" brings both humility and insight. Customs aren't museum pieces; they're part of community life, shaped by those who live them. Living communities are neighbors, not archives. Respecting boundaries, questioning sources, and holding space for many truths will prepare you for every chapter to come.

Chapter 1: A Living Thread: What Makes Celtic Folk Magic Folk

How to Read This Legacy

Now that we've established what this book covers—and what it doesn't—let's explore how to engage with these traditions thoughtfully. The path forward asks for more than curiosity: it calls for care, self-awareness, and a willingness to learn with respect. As you continue through these pages, you'll find strategies to help you move beyond surface-level excitement and build a relationship with Celtic folk customs that honors their living roots.

Before you try any custom, pause and ask yourself questions about where it came from and why it mattered to the people who practiced it. Ask what need the custom addressed. Was it marking a seasonal change, protecting children, or helping a family through hardship? Practices like tying a red thread on a child's wrist weren't just decorative—they drew their meaning from the stories families told, the time of year, and the involvement of the whole community. A grandmother's hands tying the thread, her words over it, and the gathered family's attention made it powerful. When you approach such acts, look beneath the gesture and seek the reasons and relationships that gave it life. Thinking about power dynamics matters too; the difference between a blessing shared in care and one imposed through control is more than ritual—it's about trust, belonging, and consent (Ó Giolláin, 2000).

Language carries both history and emotion in Celtic contexts. Using local terms—like Irish 'Lá Fhéile Bríde' or Scottish Gaelic 'Latha Fhèill Brìghde'—shows not only respect but an acknowledgment of cultural endurance. You may not be fluent, and that's fine, but trying out the right word, listening to recordings, or learning basic greetings signals you're approaching as a guest, not a tourist—or worse, a conqueror. Many sources about these traditions come from outsiders, especially as centuries of colonialism pressed English onto Irish, Scottish, Welsh, and Breton tongues, which affected what stories got written down and whose voices are preserved (McLeod, 2022). Notice who wrote your source, who translated it, and whether there are living community voices represented. Centering books and articles from native speakers, tradition bearers, or community members keeps living heritage at the heart of your practice (Ní Dhuibhne, 2016).

Pay attention to edges, boundaries, and times of transition in the stories and rituals you encounter. Liminal moments like dawn, dusk, shorelines, doorways, or the turning of seasons—Samhain, Beltane—are when folk magic often gathers its strength. These "in-between" spaces were considered potent and sometimes risky. For example, leaving offerings at wells as the sun rises, making protective gestures over doorways during childbirth, or gathering by bonfires as one season slips into another. Customs cluster around these thresholds because they mark shifts—not only in the outside world but in our inner lives too. When someone is born, falls ill, or dies, community action and ritual intensify, echoing the sense that crossing a threshold brings everyone closer together (McNeill, 1959). Noticing liminality helps you understand why certain acts happen at precise moments and locations, so you move beyond treating folk magic as a grab-bag of random spells.

Reflective journaling helps keep your engagement honest. Use it not for grading yourself, but to stay alert to your motives and understanding. Try these prompts throughout your reading: First, ask if you're seeking "results," like guaranteed protection or success, or if you're open to the idea that folk practices often supported comfort, cohesion, and meaning, rather than working as mechanical formulas. Second, notice whose perspectives appear in your sources—is the story coming from men or women, insiders or outsiders, people with status or those on the edge? Commit to searching out missing voices and fill gaps wherever you can. Third, root yourself in your own daily life. How might the principles of attentive reciprocity, local connection, and gentle curiosity shape your approach without borrowing customs that don't fit your circumstances? Return to these questions as companions, not hurdles, and let them help you grow a practice that fits you and respects others (Butler, 1998).

These reading strategies will serve you well as we turn to the historical landscapes and regional distinctions of Chapter 2, where Irish, Scottish, Welsh, and Breton traditions each come into clearer focus. With each chapter, bring respect, attentiveness, and openness—to the land, the languages, and the people who have shaped these living threads.

Bringing It All Together

Looking back at where we've been in this chapter, we've uncovered how folk practices find their meaning in everyday moments and local traditions. The magic here isn't separated from daily life, but shaped by it—woven into the way people sweep a floor, tell a story, or tie a protective knot for a child. We saw that these customs rarely come with a single rulebook; instead, they change to fit the needs of each place and time. They're passed along through stories, careful watching, and a willingness to adapt when circumstances shift. What holds everything together is the sense of relationship—between people, places, and the unseen world—and the value placed on sharing, memory, and respect within families and communities.

As you reflect on the patterns described, it's clear that authentic practice isn't about copying acts exactly as they were done before. It's about understanding why those acts mattered, and listening closely to the voices and stories behind them. Whether you're drawn to a small gesture or a bigger tradition, curiosity mixed with humility opens the door to meaningful connection. These traditions ask us to slow down, pay attention, and honor both our own roots and those who came before. As you move forward, keep noticing the little details in your environment and relationships—these are where enchantment often begins.

Chapter 2: Peoples and Times: Historical Roots and Regional Frames

Ideas we call "Celtic" didn't stay still; they traveled with people, languages, and trade from the Iron Age right through the early medieval period. Cultures like Hallstatt and La Tène spread their influence across Europe's seas and mountains. While Roman borders pushed into areas where Brittonic languages were spoken, Ireland stood apart, developing Goidelic learning and monastic art that found its way back to Britain and the Continent. This movement wasn't just about goods but about stories, languages, and customs crossing paths in lively exchange.

By the twelfth century, written lives of saints, law codes, and local tales show communities balancing power from overlords with kinship duties and the rhythms of seasonal work. These societies kept their unique voices alive through stories and traditions even as they adapted to change. Seeing how these different timelines and influences intertwined helps us understand Celtic identities formed across Ireland, Scotland, Wales, and Brittany—and sets the groundwork for exploring how place, language, and culture connect in this chapter.

Mapping Celtic Identities

Centuries of migration, trade, and transformation shaped the mosaic of folk practices that people today call "Celtic." To understand how these historical pressures shaped traditions, it helps to start with language. The ancient Celts were never a single group speaking one language; instead, two main branches grew over time. Goidelic includes Irish (Gaeilge), Scottish Gaelic (Gàidhlig), and Manx (Gaelg). Brittonic covers Welsh (Cymraeg), Breton (Brezhoneg), and Cornish (Kernewek) (2025). These are not relics—many communities speak, teach, and revive them today, weaving both old manuscripts and living stories into everyday life.

The differences between the two branches aren't just about words—they reveal whole ways of seeing the world. For example, in Goidelic languages the original Indo-European sound "kw" survived as a "c" or "k," while in Brittonic it became "p," so four is "ceithir" in Scottish Gaelic but "pedwar" in Welsh (Grokipedia, 1970). Ogham stones, rising along the roadsides of southwest Ireland and parts of Britain, carry the oldest written records of Irish, using a script of notches and lines carved for kinship claims and memorials. These inscriptions show forms like "MAQI" for "son" and preserve tribal names, acting as direct evidence of who lived where and what matters they named (Grokipedia, 1970). Meanwhile, Latin-script texts from monks and poets preserved Welsh and Breton tales,

Chapter 2: Peoples and Times: Historical Roots and Regional Frames

anchoring each tradition in place and time. Revivals today lean on archived stories and local lore, helping diaspora communities and newer learners reclaim connections, with appreciation for both scholarly and oral roots (2025).

Moving around the coasts and rivers, Celtic-speaking peoples traded, married, and shared ideas across what is now Ireland, Britain, and Brittany. The Irish Sea and Armorican coast were busy routes for salt, hides, wine, and metalwork, but also for beliefs, tunes, and woven patterns. A spiral pattern in metal jewelry might show up in Cork, then again in mid-Wales, each reimagined in new colors. Traveling craftspeople and wandering holy people, known as peregrini, carried rituals and tales as they went—from healing charms against storms to stories of miraculous cattle. These cultural carriers spread both shared motifs and sparks of difference: as traditions collided or adapted to new climates and rulers, festivals, music, and rituals took on flavors unique to their regions (2025; Grokipedia, 1970).

Welcoming Christianity did not erase older ways, but layered them with new meanings. Many early churches rose beside sacred wells, stones, or groves—places already honored by local people—so that saints' blessings could protect landscapes deeply tied to ancestral memory. Monasteries set out calendars blending Christian feasts with sowing, shearing, and harvest days, letting rural families mark familiar seasonal changes through prayers or processions. Hagiographies—the lives of saints—retold tales of heroic contests, journeys to holy wells, and protection from ill fortune, keeping echoes of myth inside church walls. St. Brigid's well remains a site where offerings and prayers meet, showing how practices found continuity beneath shifting beliefs. These themes will return in later chapters when exploring the rhythm of festivals, plant lore, and protective rites (2025; Grokipedia, 1970).

Community boundaries and shared place-lore supported a sense of belonging that ran deeper than distant rulers. Parish stones, river crossings, and guardian hills told stories about cattle raids, kinship triumphs, and oaths sworn on sacred ground. Seasonal rituals like walking parish limits—sometimes marking boundaries with rods, sometimes blessing fields at a spring—reminded everyone whose care protected the land. Though abbeys and lords bargained for power, local customs kept everyday sovereignty alive in household blessings, neighborly gatherings, and small gifts to streams or trees. Today, honoring these living distinctions means listening for regional voices and respecting boundaries—an ethical stance that will echo in the chapter on engagement and care. These language families and regional identities were lived out through daily relationships, work, and celebration, which shaped the kinship bonds and social structures explored next (2025; Grokipedia, 1970).

Society, Law, and Daily Life

Having traced how language families and monastic networks shaped Celtic identities, we now turn to the social structures that carried these identities through daily life. The regional variations mapped—Goidelic and Brittonic, coastal trade and monastic travel—were lived through webs of kinship, custom, work, and craftsmanship. In this world, communal bonds, household rhythms, and the rules that governed them shaped not just survival but the ways folk knowledge and magical acts were shared, authorized, and remembered (aihowells, 2025).

Kinship set the boundaries of belonging. Families organized themselves by blood, marriage, and a practice called fosterage: sending children to be raised in another household, creating ties that bound communities beyond simple ancestry. Fosterage was both practical and strategic; it built trust between rival households, linked distant valleys, and laid pathways for sharing remedies, charms, and weather wisdom. For instance, when a midwife fostered a herder's daughter, she didn't just pass on skills privately. Remedies for difficult births flowed uphill with visiting shepherds, and signs for lambing weather drifted back down with the returning child. These social exchanges meant folk magic was always communal, never hidden away in isolation.

Genealogies did more than trace who belonged where; they decided which elders led rituals, who blessed water at births, and whose cattle received first protections. Attendance at threshold blessings or harvest feasts wasn't simply who happened to be closest, but woven into layers of alliance and obligation. When an elder midwife or seasoned boat-builder performed a charm or named a taboo, their authority came directly from these webs of connection—every spell, blessing, or ban was carried by a network of memories and relationships that gave it weight. Marriage ties and fosterage dictated who held responsibility for protective rites, so skills and stories traveled reliably along familiar paths. This kept folk practices living, open to renewal as new hands took up old words.

Community rules—what we call Brehon law in Ireland—structured daily interactions, giving everyday speech and action powerful meaning. Everyone had an honor-price: a recognized value attached to their place in society. When someone gave an oath, pronounced a curse, or offered a spoken blessing, those words mattered because breaking or honoring them affected not just reputation but tangible standing in the community. A blessing for safe calving or a curse upon a spoiled well might be backed by sureties—people who stood witness and vouched for truth. Community members didn't just see magic as private belief; they understood that spoken formulas carried legal and social consequence (aihowells, 2025). Witness rituals, marks, and even satiric verses made truth public and personal. Satire—the art of shaming through sharp words—was itself a form of protection that could ruin a reputation if someone ignored communal taboos, giving spoken charms real teeth.

Customary remedies usually expected restitution and ritual apology when someone broke a boundary or harmed another's property, whether accidentally or not. If a neighbor crossed a boundary hedge without permission, setting things right required more than words. The offender might return tools, recite a charm of reconciliation, and offer practical help at the next communal workday. This blend of law and healing meant that repair in the community was as much about restoring balance and trust as about fixing the physical damage. In these ways, law became a living bridge to ritual, showing everyone that daily acts—words spoken, actions witnessed—had material, social, and magical consequence.

Seasonal labor anchored these structures to cycles of work and need. Transhumance—the seasonal movement of livestock to distant pastures—marked moments when both animals and humans needed extra protection. Before families drove cattle to summer grazing, they blessed gates, sprinkled water on thresholds, and recited protective charms for beasts and herders alike. Livelihoods rode on the success of fishing runs and harvests, so timing was everything. Quarter days and cross-quarter celebrations, like Beltane and Samhain, marked not just holidays but coordination points when whole communities acted together. On these days, household blessings mixed with gatherings for swapping news, trading goods, and confirming alliances. Weather lore and moon phases guided crops and peat-cutting; cutting turf on the waxing moon wasn't only luck, it helped fuel dry quicker, marrying observation with blessing.

These kinship webs and seasonal labor patterns will help explain why certain protections cluster around thresholds and livestock—themes we'll explore in Chapter 7's household customs. Craftwork was no less attuned to community rhythms. Trades like smithing or weaving preserved family secrets as shared professional knowledge, often clothed in taboos and auspicious days. A smith's refusal to fire the forge on certain saints' days mirrored community festival calendars, connecting quality and safety with devotion and rest. Harbor cooperatives and local guilds coordinated feast-day obligations and the blessing of nets or tools, ensuring that craft and faith moved hand in hand. Calendars for starting big projects weren't just mystical—they matched times when neighbors gathered and extra hands were available, making even ordinary workdays part of the wider social choreography. These rituals wove protective power and professional pride together, keeping both people and products safe while honoring shared values (aihowells, 2025).

With daily patterns established, turn to how Christian institutions braided with older customs to shape shared spaces and times.

Christianity and Continuity

The kinship networks, seasonal labor rhythms, and craft traditions shaping everyday life across Celtic regions became the very roots into which Christianity settled. Parish churches, monastic houses, and feast days threaded themselves through cycles of sowing, shearing, and harvest fairs already defined by kin-based responsibility and communal gathering. Rather than sweeping away local customs, early Christian leaders often met tradition midway, adapting devotions to language and landmarks people already loved. That pattern set the stage for a living synthesis rather than a sharp divide between old and new ways (Venutius, 2024).

Chapter 2: Peoples and Times: Historical Roots and Regional Frames

Saints in these landscapes rarely stood apart from place; instead, their stories were mapped onto freshwater springs, high ridges, or coastal promontories crucial to local identity. St. Brigid's wells in Ireland draw thousands for ritual circuits and water-taking every February; these processions follow the sunwise path, echoing older patterns of veneration linked to fertility and protection. In Wales, St. Winifred's Well at Holywell is famed for healing, as are countless lesser sites— each with its own blend of offering coins, tying rags to nearby trees, and returning each year on the saint's feast day. These practices kept community memory anchored in land and water, even as Church narratives reframed ancient guardians as saints (Venutius, 2024). Pilgrimage itself adapted, mirroring earlier devotion where journeying to a sacred feature strengthened ties between neighbors, place, and the wider world. The stories that survived remind us: devotion was always lived locally, not just preached from afar.

Blessings and protections moved fluidly between lay households and ordained clergy. In many homes, threshold-sweeping prayers, livestock charms, and fishing boat blessings wound together formulas remembered from generations past. A mother might sprinkle holy water while asking Mary's protection on her children, tracing the sign of the cross over doorways or cattle. Priestly rites—weddings, burials, or mass— had formal power, but lay practices thrived in parallel, sometimes skirting official approval when they echoed older meanings with Christian words. Where church authorities disapproved or tried to suppress certain acts, families often changed the language but preserved the structure and intent.

The same charm for warding off sickness or securing a safe journey might swap out the name of a river goddess for that of a patron saint or Angel Michael (*A Pagan's Perspective: Critiques of Christianity*, 2024; Venutius, 2024).

Building on the patterns of market fairs and seasonal gatherings, Christian feasts became social fulcrums timed to local needs. Candlemas, Lammas, and All Saints' Day coincided with spring beginnings, first harvests, or post-reaping rest. Easter arrived as lambs filled fields and days lengthened; Christmas fell soon after the winter solstice, bringing hope and celebration as food stores ran low and the promise of light returned. These overlapping cycles made faith practical as well as spiritual. Advent fasts and Lenten abstinence fit the realities of larders before abundance, while festival eves brought bonfires, processionals, and midnight vigils blurring sacred hours into workaday life. Even when the calendar's reasons changed, the shared sense of time—of preparation, risk, and renewal—remained steady, keeping communal bonds strong (*A Pagan's Perspective: Critiques of Christianity*, 2024).

Material culture reveals how layers of meaning accumulated quietly. Crosses inscribed atop older standing stones signaled ongoing guardianship of place, not erasure. At hearths, Brigid's crosses woven from rushes marked Imbolc and St. Brigid's Day, protecting homes while blessing the threshold of spring. Relics and banners for local saints traveled in processions marked with rowan or hawthorn branches, linking Christian hope with plant lore and boundary magic described elsewhere in this book. Floral garlands on church doors in Brittany or Scotland often worked double-duty, both honoring saints and maintaining a living connection with earth's cycles. These objects show that images and gestures might change form, but their purpose—to protect, remember, and root communities in place—endured (Venutius, 2024).

Recognizing these syncretic layers helps readers step beyond the idea of a "pure" pre-Christian practice or a uniform Christianity. Traditions explored in later chapters—pilgrim routes, protective charms, household rituals—reflect an active weaving of belief and belonging. Blessings spoken over tools, crossings tracked at ancient wells, and festival meals all carry echoes of adaptation and memory. Having shown the braid of devotion and custom, we must now examine the sources that shape our understanding—and their silences. The next section looks more closely at hagiographies, parish records, and folklore collections, uncovering how evidence itself shapes the stories we inherit.

Sources and Silences

Having explored how Christian devotion and folk custom wove together, we must now ask: how do we know what we know? Every story, ritual, and blessing we've discussed reached us through collectors, clerks, and chroniclers who shaped what survived—and what disappeared. This understanding rests not only on surviving customs but also on the way they were recorded, filtered, or sometimes lost along the way.

Collector's Lens: Victorian Filters and Romanticism

Nineteenth-century folklorists traveled the British Isles searching for the "ancient" traditions of Celtic peoples. Driven by romantic nationalism and a hunger for lost ages, these collectors gathered stories from rural communities, but often favored colorful legends over humble practices. Dialects were translated into literary English, and repetitive or contradictory details—and most domestic rituals—were smoothed away to fit what outsiders expected from "real" folk culture. For instance, a charm used to protect cattle might be written down, yet its subtle rules—the need to speak it before sunrise or never recite it aloud on Tuesdays—could vanish. The collector might have dismissed such restrictions as mere superstition, giving readers only part of the living picture. This doesn't mean the sources should be discarded. Knowing their backgrounds lets us value the glimpses they offer without taking them as unfiltered truth (Bennett, 1991). When we approach collections of charms, fairy tales, and song with an eye for what has been left out, we start honoring both the tradition and the people who carried it in daily life.

Legal Records: Witch Trial Documents and Their Distortions

Court documents and witch trial records seem at first like solid evidence. They contain names, dates, accusations, and even quoted confessions. Yet these accounts echo the fears and formulaic thinking of their time more than they capture everyday belief. Confessions of cursing, healing, or meeting fairies almost always came after repeated questioning, threats, or torture. The language of trials features Latin phrases, theological arguments, and long lists of forbidden acts that frame accused people as criminals rather than neighbors. What emerges is less a map of real-world practice than a tapestry of anxiety about disorder and power (Levack, 2016). Amid these distortions, familiar themes appear: protections with iron, secret exchanges between neighbors, concern for crops and animals. These recurring motifs, when compared with other records or lived memories, hint at the ordinary uses of magic under extraordinary pressure. Reading such documents means treating them as windows onto community stress, not neutral mirrors of the past.

Ethnography Ethics: Who Told the Story, and to Whom?

Fieldwork in folklore often looks like a university-trained visitor arriving with notebook in hand, hoping to capture stories. Power sits in the background of every exchange. The visiting folklorist holds status and shapes what appears "worth collecting." Local narrators make choices about what to share, keep private, exaggerate, or downplay. A midwife might describe a birthing charm but leave out private remedies known only within her family. A young farmhand may tell tales about field blessings while avoiding discussion of household secrets meant only for elders. Each person's age, job, gender, and standing influence what forms of knowledge are available to outsiders. Often, women's voices, laborers' experiences, the songs of travelers and marginalized groups go missing from published collections. If we start comparing stories across different places, ages, and professions, patterns emerge—and so do gaps. Part of responsibly reading folk sources is noticing who is absent as much as who is present (Ó Giolláin, 2000).

As you move forward into chapters on seasonal practices and sacred plants, this awareness of sources will help you distinguish living tradition from invented romance—and approach customs with the respect they deserve. The ethical lens from the beginning of this book, and the cautions you'll encounter about appropriation later, call us to hold space for the real lives behind the lore.

Reading Against the Grain: Strategies for Cautious Interpretation

When you look at the "evidence" of folk magic, it's helpful to put official narratives beside local clues. Annals and saints' lives give broad frames; place-names, old fair dates, or archaeological traces root customs in their settings. Notice what's not being said: if women's daily work barely appears in legal codes but survives in family prayers, consider why. Sometimes secrecy kept a practice alive because it was too private, taboo, or ordinary to record. Before taking any ritual as a blanket "Celtic" custom, pause to ask what it achieved for those who did it, right there and then. For example, walking boundaries at Beltane might settle land disputes one year, or bless livestock another, depending on local tensions and needs. With each source, stay curious about both voice and silence. Respectful reading means cross-checking stories, listening for quiet details, and handling inherited beliefs with care—for their sake, and for ours.

Source criticism isn't just academic nitpicking—it builds trust and self-confidence for anyone seeking connection with folk tradition. Each time we weigh a tale's gaps or a ritual's likely edits, we're learning alongside ancestors and neighbors. We honor their creativity, their struggles, and the imperfect archives they've left behind. These skills aren't about casting doubt; they're about making space for honesty and relationship. As you journey into the next chapters—exploring seasons, landscapes, and the heart of household practice—you carry tools for discernment, curiosity, and humility. This is the bedrock of ethical folk magic, rooted in respect for both story and source.

References: Bennett, M. (1991). "Folk and Fairy Tales of the British Isles." Oxford University Press. Levack, B. P. (2016). "The Witch-Hunt in Early Modern Europe." Routledge. Ó Giolláin, D. (2000). "Locating Irish Folklore: Tradition, Modernity, Identity." Cork University Press.

Bringing It All Together

This chapter has traveled across centuries and landscapes, following the threads that connect languages, stories, and customs often grouped under the name "Celtic." We saw how these ideas took root in Brittonic and Goidelic language families, moved with trade and migration, and adapted as Christianity mingled with older traditions. From river crossings marked by shared tales to monastic scribes translating poetry, every community found ways to keep their sense of belonging alive. Whether through laws shaped by kinship, songs passed at the hearth, or rituals anchoring the year's rhythms, people shaped their own forms of protection, celebration, and connection.

By looking at how layers of influence—Roman borders, Irish scholarship, Christian practice, local law—wove together, we start to see Celtic identity not as a fixed label, but as something flexible and alive. These identities survived pressures from both outside empires and local rulers because they found strength in daily life, practical needs, and cherished places. Understanding this helps us honor the living roots behind names and customs, and it gives us tools for exploring our own connections to tradition—always with care, curiosity, and respect. As you continue reading, these braided timelines and lived practices offer a richer way to approach folk magic, ancestry, and a sense of place in today's world.

Chapter 3: Speaking with the Land: Place, Spirit, and Reciprocity

It's easy to think of land as just a backdrop for our lives—a space to be used, owned, or shaped by human hands. We often picture fields waiting to be farmed, hills to be climbed, or resources ready for the taking. But if we pause and listen to old stories, sayings, and village traditions from Celtic culture, a different picture emerges. These sources reveal a deeper connection where land isn't just something out there; it's like family. The earth, rivers, and trees were seen as living beings—neighbors to greet, thank, and even ask for guidance. This way of thinking invites us to hear land in terms of relationship instead of possession.

When we put aside ideas about owning or controlling the land, we begin to notice how daily actions become gentle conversations rather than orders shouted into empty space. This perspective invites us to slow down and ask: What would it mean to live alongside a place, respecting its needs and presence? In these pages, we'll explore how this idea of kinship shaped customs, stories, and everyday care. By opening ourselves to the land as a living relation, we can learn new ways to connect that honor kindness, respect, and shared life, offering a fresh view on what it truly means to belong somewhere.

Beyond Ownership to Kinship

In Chapter 1, we saw how Celtic folk magic operated through relationships rather than commands—now we turn to the most fundamental relationship of all: the bond between people and place. Within this framework, land was not a possession to be parceled or drained for private use. People understood themselves as part of a living world filled with neighbors—some human, some not—each deserving recognition, gratitude, and reciprocity. Fields, rivers, stones, and trees were described in story and custom as persons with personalities, temperaments, and needs. This kinship worldview shaped every custom, story, and gesture connected to survival and thriving.

Hospitality was a sacred duty that extended beyond the household door. The tradition held that welcoming a guest—whether stranger, animal, or spirit—meant opening oneself to blessing as well as risk. Folktales from Ireland, Scotland, Wales, and Brittany tell of those who turned away travelers or neglected to share food, only to find their crops blighted or luck turned (Ó hÓgáin, 1991). Bread and fire offered to a hungry wanderer also recognized the presence of spirits and the land itself; the hearth became a meeting ground for visible and invisible kin. When milk, butter, or bread was shared at

Chapter 3: Speaking with the Land: Place, Spirit, and Reciprocity

key seasons—or placed on windowsills for the "good neighbors"—it marked a cycle where giving and receiving kept abundance moving within the whole network (Evans-Wentz, 1911). Modern readers may see echoes of this ethic in simple acts like caring for a local park, sharing garden produce, or acknowledging the more-than-human company one keeps outside.

A walk to a spring or an old tree often called for a word of thanks or a small gesture. Offerings could be as simple as returning a sip of water to the source after drinking, placing a pebble at a standing stone, threading a strip of cloth—a clootie—on a tree's branch, or leaving behind a pinch of oatmeal. These tokens weren't extravagant or showy but matched the humility of the moment. They served as signals of acknowledgment, formed more as conversations than bargains (McNeill, 1956). The land and its spirits were treated as hosts with whom one built trust over time. Spoken words might be barely above a whisper, yet considered heard by those meant to receive them. Compared with modern practices that sometimes bring crowds, plastic trinkets, or large offerings to well-known sacred sites, these older customs offer models of scale and care: biodegradable, minimal, present without claiming.

Boundaries held special weight in this worldview. A gate, stile, or even a change in soil underfoot signaled a crossing—not just of property, but into another's sphere of care. Announcing oneself was common: a greeting, a pause, a hat tipped or hand raised. Entering a field or woods might call for a verbal request or a physical sign, such as closing a gate or staying to established paths. Gathering herbs involved seeking permission, whether silently or aloud, and harvesting only what could be spared (Graves, 1961). These practices made explicit the understanding that every threshold represented cooperation—not just with other humans, but with the wider family of place-spirits believed to guard fields, rivers, and gates. Consent here was practical and direct. It prevented harm, misunderstandings, and ensured goodwill between those whose lives overlapped, both seen and unseen.

Care extended into land management itself. Rotational grazing allowed grass and soil to recover, giving the land what people described as time to "breathe" (Foster, 2000). Hedgerows, tangled with birds and brambles, were pruned with attention and rarely destroyed. They offered homes to wildlife while also acting as boundaries respected by people and, in tradition, the spirits who safeguarded each side. Taboos against cutting certain trees or drawing water from springs during specific times reflected both ecological insight and reverence (MacNeill, 1959). Some spots needed protection, especially during nesting or recovery seasons. Ancient stewardship practices grew out of careful observation and accumulated wisdom; sustainability was woven directly into moral action. This land-as-kin perspective shaped everything from daily greetings at gates to seasonal plant gathering—practices we'll explore in depth when we turn to herbs and hedgerows in Chapter 5.

Today, recognizing patterns of kinship-thinking helps us read the historical record and folktale collections with fresh eyes. What might once have seemed quaint or superstitious emerges as practical wisdom adapted to real conditions—survival in a landscape full of agency and memory. Hospitality, thanksgiving, consent, and stewardship stand revealed not as ceremony for ceremony's sake, but as guidelines for living alongside others who shape our lives. Having reframed land as kin, we now turn to where and when this kinship is most strongly felt: at thresholds of place and time, where boundaries blur and presence intensifies.

Liminal Places and Times

Having reframed land as kin, we now turn to where and when that kinship is most keenly felt. In Celtic folk traditions, thresholds—those places and times that rest between worlds—stand out as moments of sharpened awareness and care. Folk custom centers on the recognition that boundaries, whether along a path or in the flow of time, are not simply separators; they are places of encounter and negotiation. This is where the ethic of hospitality toward both land and spirit becomes visible, setting the stage for many everyday acts of courtesy and caution.

Between Worlds: Why Edges Heighten Presence and Potency

Edges such as dawn, dusk, shorelines, hilltops, and river fords create a kind of pause. At these points, categories blur—the dark recedes but the full day has not yet arrived, or the land gives way to water with no hard line between. Standing at a shoreline in Connemara, a person might notice how the sound of waves merges with the call of seabirds, creating an atmosphere neither wholly marine nor fully part of the fields behind them (Ó Giolláin, 2000). Stories tell of fishers leaving a piece of bread or saying a quiet word before pushing out to sea, recognizing that the edge where sand meets tide belongs to neither party alone. Dawn and dusk hold this same ambiguity; light softens and shadows stretch, making it feel natural to pause, greet the coming or departing day, and offer a blessing or caution depending on what tasks lie ahead (Evans-Wentz, 1911). Hilltops and fords appear often in tales as meeting points for messages, omens, or warnings, joining together two landscapes and serving as gathering spots for travelers, spirits, or weather changes.

When moving from field to field or crossing a stile, greetings—sometimes as simple as "God save all here"—signal respect for whatever, or whoever, might be sharing the threshold with you. There is an understanding that what sits at the edge holds watch over both sides. In Irish and Scottish custom alike, people heightened their attention and courtesy at these crossings, believing good manners protected against misfortune or offense (Ó Crualaoich, 2003).

Chapter 3: Speaking with the Land: Place, Spirit, and Reciprocity

Festival Doors: Samhain and Beltane as Temporal Crossings

Thresholds in time are just as powerful as those in landscape. The turning of seasons opens 'doors' felt by entire communities. During Samhain, which marks the beginning of winter, households tended the hearth fire carefully, honored ancestors, and avoided traveling after dark. Stories from County Kerry recall families banking the fire and sweeping the doorstep before nightfall, a gesture rooted in managing what entered the home as the season changed (Danaher, 1972). People carried food outdoors to share with neighbors or left dishes set for unseen guests, reinforcing the idea that kindness at the door kept blessings near and trouble away.

Beltane, arriving with May, brought a different set of customs focused on protection and safe passage into the growing season. Cattle were driven between bonfires to shield them from illness, houses were decorated with green branches, and all who lived within a household joined in greeting the new rush of life (MacNeill, 1959). These practices, far from superstition, reflect thoughtful management of what crosses in and out through temporal thresholds—acts not of fear, but of responsibility toward community and land alike. The shape of these festivals reminds us that just as physical edges demand care, so do the hinges of the year.

Crossroads Etiquette: Protocols and Perils in Folk Tales

In Irish and Welsh storytelling, crossroads are charged not only with possibility but also with risk. Where paths cross, encounters multiply—people, stories, strangers, and spirits might all pass at once. Folktales warn against boasting or lingering at such intersections, especially after dark, teaching humility and swift passage. Protective tokens in the pocket or a pinch of salt cast quietly to the side help mark one's own safety while signaling deference to any presence encountered (Briggs, 1976). Naming certain beings aloud is avoided, as words have power and can invite attention.

Leaving small offerings—a coin tucked behind a stone or a crumb off the main path—signals respect. These gestures resemble the politeness shown in a stranger's house: acknowledgment, gratitude, and carefulness form the backbone of protocol. Readers might see these customs less as superstition and more as practical social sense, much like observing etiquette in unfamiliar situations today.

Tide and Mist: Maritime Liminality in Scottish and Breton Lore

Tide and mist on the Atlantic coasts bring their own lessons about living with uncertainty. In Scottish and Breton fishing villages, the shifting line of the sea was a daily reminder of the world's changeability. Those heading out at dawn watched moon and tide closely—not only for safety, but to match their timing with the moods of sea-spirits believed to dwell beyond the surf (McNeill, 1956). Fog meant lowering voices and moving with extra caution; to call too loudly risked bringing confusion or inviting otherworldly attention when visibility shrank to only a few feet. Harbor rites such as touching a stone at the pierhead or saluting a headland marked entry into another element's care, an unspoken agreement to respect whatever governed those waters.

The lived experience of maritime liminality could be stark—a sudden fogbank swallowing up sight, or the tide turning beneath a boat and urging quick decisions. Customs that accompanied these moments arose from real need, but also from kinship with forces larger than oneself. Watching for changing currents, honoring invisible boundaries, and practicing quiet respect became forms of both survival and relationship with place.

Edges invite encounters; recognizing them prepares us to meet well. Thresholds in Celtic tradition are sites of heightened presence and attentiveness, drawing forward the etiquette that will guide us as we learn about the neighbors met at those edges next.

Guardians and Neighbors Unseen

Having explored the thresholds where encounters might occur, we now turn to who tradition said dwelled in those spaces. At crossroads, shorelines, and festival nights, Celtic folk traditions taught that the land was not empty but shared with an unseen company. These neighbors went by many titles—Good People, Fair Folk, Themselves—a language shaped as much by caution as courtesy. Naming them kindly or obliquely helped keep peace, since open naming could signal disrespect or invite unwanted attention. Encounters with such beings were expected at liminal places and times (Briggs, 1976). Daily life wove their presence into routine; they were as real as any human neighbor, and the etiquette for relating to them ran parallel too.

Everyday practices reflected a careful balance of hospitality and distance. Offerings were simple: a splash of milk at the doorstep, a pinch of oatmeal left where paths crossed, a thimbleful of honey on a stone. These gestures were never extravagant or frequent; giving too much or too often risked creating a sense of obligation or debt, which could upset the delicate terms of neighborliness (Evans-Wentz, 1911). Spirits did not serve people; rather, both sides respected boundaries. Limiting requests, leaving wild places undisturbed, and keeping personal needs modest were ways of showing respect for autonomy on all sides. These naming practices reflect the relational worldview introduced in Chapter 1, where respect flows through right relationship rather than command or control. Words mattered, but so did acts—hearing thank-you murmured at a well or noticing a crumb left at a boundary made these relationships tangible.

Folklore overflows with tales warning against careless exchange. Accepting food or fire from unknown hands, especially at liminal hours or sites, did more than satisfy hunger or light a hearth—it brought invisible strings. Such exchanges might create a bond that lingered, drawing someone into trouble or mischief if accepted without blessing or proper context (Ó hÓgáin, 2006). Stories caution against taking a bite of bread offered by a stranger near a fairy mound after dark, or lighting a candle from a mysterious ember at a crossroads; the line between kindness and entanglement was razor thin. By contrast, open borrowing among known neighbors followed set etiquette: requests spoken aloud, thanks given in full view, and sometimes token gifts returned to make the accounting clear. When in doubt, refusing gently or offering a blessing kept accounts clean, echoing the broader theme that gratitude and transparency defined safe community—for seen and unseen neighbors alike.

At night, when households felt most exposed and thresholds most uncertain, families turned to protections grounded in daily objects. Iron in the form of a nail above the door or a knife under a pillow was believed to deter wandering spirits— less aggression, more a gentle signal to keep away (Briggs, 1976). Salt, scattered across entryways or sprinkled in cottage corners, acted as both purifier and boundary marker, reflecting its practical role as preserver as much as symbolic shield. Travelers carrying water blessed by a local priest, a sprig of rowan tied with red thread, or a memorized prayer for crossing moors and fords, placed their trust in layers of ritual learned at home, passed from grandparent to child (McNeill, 1956). The knowledge stayed close to daily life—no need for secret knowledge, just steady practice rooted in familiar things.

Language carried as much weight as physical gesture. Local names mattered, shaping how one spoke about both place and presence. Irish storytellers called the hidden folk the Good People; Scots preferred Themselves or the People of Peace; the Welsh used Tylwyth Teg with careful exactness (Ó hÓgáin, 2006). Each term expressed its own etiquette, echoed in countless small taboos: not whistling near certain old trees, avoiding a pointed finger aimed at a fairy hill, singing only approved melodies at the well. Even within a single valley, phrases might shift—what held true for one household might be quietly altered by the next. Asking local elders how to "speak about" a spring or hillside offered both vocabulary and a lesson in humility. Honoring such variety is part of ethical engagement, a theme returned to in Chapter 9: respectful connection means learning the living customs rather than assuming one term fits all. These customs taught care not only in words but in deeds, reinforcing kinship over command.

Understanding these categories and cautions sets the stage for the practical reciprocity strategies that translate reverence into everyday action. In the next section, each reader will find steps for greeting, thanking, and sharing space with unseen neighbors, turning awareness into reliable habits.

Chapter 3: Speaking with the Land: Place, Spirit, and Reciprocity

Reciprocity in Practice

Having established respectful distance with guardians and place-spirits, the next step is bringing that same mindfulness to visible places and living communities. Kinship with land comes alive through steady gestures—regular, real-world actions that reach beyond abstract ideas or well-intentioned feelings. As you walk a local path or linger near a stream, each small choice—how you tread, whom you greet, what you leave behind—shapes this relationship.

A good way to begin is simple observation. Before any gifts or rituals, devote yourself to listening. Every landscape speaks its own language, not in words but in subtle signs—a shift in birdsong at dusk, the clean scent after rain, the return of swallows in spring. To cultivate this attention, pick one route close to home: a city riverbank, park footpath, or quiet hedgerow. Visit at dawn and dusk for four weeks. Each time, jot down three sensory details in a pocket notebook: maybe the sharp cry of a jay, how brambles curl by the water, or dew beading on spiderwebs. Over days, patterns emerge: which birds call before sunrise, when the first frosts bite, which wildflowers bloom together. Tracking these details—migration dates, bud-break, water clarity—helps you meet the land as an active presence, not just scenery (Beresford Ellis, 1999; Ní Dhuibhne, 1992). Waiting a full month before offering anything physical teaches humility. It reduces risk of misstep, letting the landscape reveal what suits it best instead of imposing your own expectations.

Human consent matters no less than spirit permission. Fields, woods, and shorelines often carry layers of stewardship. Seek permission from farmers, private owners, or indigenous leaders before venturing off public paths. This is both law and spiritual courtesy, echoing the consent-based approach at the core of living Celtic tradition (Ó Crualaoich, 2003). You might say, "I'm hoping to walk quietly along the south field to observe seasonal changes. I'll visit once or twice a week for about half an hour each time. Would this be all right?" Honor their boundaries. Stick to agreed paths, never trample crops, close each gate, and keep clear of livestock. Show gratitude by collecting stray litter, letting folks know if you spot a broken fence, or leaving a handwritten thank-you. These are not payments for entry, but gentle ways to give back, enacting reciprocity with every visit (McNeill, 1957).

The question of offerings arises quickly. Traditions recall milk poured on stones, flowers laid at wells, or coins slipped into tree roots. While older customs used only natural, biodegradable things, plastic ribbons and metal coins now clutter many sacred places, harming soil and polluting rivers. Consider ephemeral offerings: pour a cup of clean water at a spring, sing a quiet song, or light a beeswax candle briefly—always taking everything home afterward. If you feel called to leave something tangible, choose small petals from abundant wildflowers or a short length of wool thread that will vanish in weather. Steer clear of plastics, pennies, glass beads, or anything synthetic. What looks like beauty today can become tangled waste tomorrow, burdening the very land you hoped to honor (Beresford Ellis, 1999).

These practices model the book's broader ethics as explored later—modest, context-aware choices that place care above performance. Rather than following rules for their own sake, the heart of kinship is ongoing dialogue. Ask yourself: Would this place benefit more from my silent company than anything I could offer? Do my regular visits disturb shy deer or ground-nesting birds? Can I help protect this patch by volunteering for a cleanup, learning its stories, or correcting misinformation? Sometimes true honoring means picking up fishing line or writing a letter of thanks to local caretakers. Let gratitude ripple beyond ritual, drawing you into action—supporting conservation, thanking farm workers, or helping others see the living history within each hedgerow.

Concluding Thoughts

As we look back at what we've explored here, one message stands out: the Celtic approach to land was never about ownership or command. Instead, people saw themselves as living among relatives—where rivers, stones, and fields held their own voices and needs. From simple greetings at a gate to quiet offerings by a spring, these gestures come from a deep sense of kinship and mutual respect. The old stories and customs invite us to see land not as something separate to be controlled, but as an active partner in daily life—a partner that listens, responds, and even teaches if we're willing to slow down and pay attention.

When we shift away from habits of possession and listen for connection, our ordinary routines begin to feel more like conversations than demands. This way of relating runs deeper than ritual; it asks us to show up with humility, gratitude, and care every day. Whether you're pausing at a crossroads, tending a backyard garden, or walking through city parks, these small acts echo the spirit of kinship valued by Celtic folk magic. Moving forward, each mindful step offers a chance to practice belonging—with each other, with the invisible neighbors of place, and with the land itself.

Chapter 4: The Turning Year: Seasonal Rhythms and Folk Calendars

In early medieval Ireland, people didn't just note big events like plagues, eclipses, or kingly deaths; they also carefully recorded the hardships of everyday life—failed harvests and freezing winters. These early annalists were showing us something important: keeping track of time wasn't just about marking sacred days or religious ritual—it was essential for making it through the year. Long before clocks and printed calendars, communities spread across Ireland, Scotland, Wales, and Brittany followed the year's rhythm by watching four key quarter-days and the sun's slow dance at solstices and equinoxes. Ancient passage tombs were built to catch the winter solstice's first light, local fairs drew neighbors together at Lughnasadh, and saints' feast days blended with older seasonal traditions, weaving a calendar full of stories, memories, and practical needs.

These patterns weren't merely about counting days or celebrating—they helped shape daily life, work, and community bonds. The festivals that punctuated the year—starting with the well-known four fire festivals—served as markers of time and shared experience, connecting people to the land, each other, and their ancestors. By exploring how these cycles lived in folk life, we can better appreciate the layers of meaning behind familiar customs and how ancient peoples made sense of their changing world. This chapter invites you to step into those rhythms and understand the turning year from a perspective grounded in survival, memory, and celebration.

Four Fire Festivals Revisited

As we've seen, the turning year was felt in hearth and field alike, stitching people's lives together by the rhythms of the land. At the core of these cycles sit the four fire festivals—cornerstones for timekeeping, belief, and everyday survival. Each one helps mark not only what's next on the farm or in the village but also who belongs, who is remembered, and how the community holds firm against both change and uncertainty (ipsadmin, 2024).

Samhain: Crossing Thresholds as the Year Turns

When the last crops were gathered and evenings shrank toward cold, smoky dark, Samhain set its stamp on every household. The focus shifted to protection—small red embers from the main fire circled livestock outside, meant to ward off harm on a night when the barrier between worlds thinned. Inside, bannocks baked with care fed living and dead alike. Seats were left open at tables for loved ones gone, honoring memory with quiet respect rather than grand display. These weren't just gestures; in a world where loss hovered near, Samhain rituals worked as real-world shields against unknowns. Vigil might mean a single candle burning overnight or neighbors trading stories long after chores ended—all practical acts rooted in both need and faith. As old calendars tell us, this was year's end and beginning in one, reminding everyone that even endings bring new beginnings alongside grief (ipsadmin, 2024).

Imbolc: Kindling Hope as Light Returns

Imbolc arrives in the heart of winter's gloom, brightening kitchens and hands busy weaving Brigid's crosses out of rushes. Families craft these simple charms and hang them above doorways, blending pride in making with wishes for protection, health, and a fruitful season ahead. Honoring wells and springs—places where Brigid is said to heal—pulls people outdoors, where ribbons and clooties (strips of cloth) flutter from thorn trees beside water. At Imbolc, the sacred steps right into daily life. Brigid herself belongs to both pre-Christian and Christian traditions, standing as healer, poet, and patron of creative work. Lighting a candle in her honor fits neatly alongside bringing in the first newborn lambs or blessing tools for the coming season. Even today, some will visit holy wells, sharing silences or quiet music within sight of blooming snowdrops. While each community shapes the day its own way, Imbolc keeps the heartbeat of hope steady through darkness (ipsadmin, 2024).

Beltane: Fires, Boundaries, Blossoms in Bloom

Beltane comes alive with motion and warmth. Cattle are driven through twin bonfires, smoke curling around their flanks to keep illness and bad luck away before they head to summer pastures. Children and elders gather hawthorn blossoms—never whole branches—twining small garlands to hang on doors or across animals' pens. In many places, paths are mended and boundaries marked anew, backed by shared fires that light up crossroads and hilltops. The mood is neither wild nor reckless; there's careful attention to local custom, with each act balancing well-being and neighborly trust. Agreements between households or communities start fresh here, matching nature's own surge of growth. Underneath all this, Beltane asks everyone to notice who stands close, what ties endure, and how shared effort brings safety as well as celebration (ipsadmin, 2024).

Lughnasadh: Gathering, Gratitude, and Social Bonds

Lughnasadh signals a time for country fairs and collective thanks. Imagine fields buzzing with contests—races, games, shows of skill—while stalls offer bread from the year's first grain. Trial marriages, called handfastings, let couples publicly test the waters, often lasting a single year before being confirmed or released. Bilberries, apples, and cakes pass from hand to hand in ritual welcome. Here, gratitude moves well

Chapter 4: The Turning Year: Seasonal Rhythms and Folk Calendars

beyond private prayer, showing up in shared food, new contracts, and plenty of laughter. For those helping with harvest, Lughnasadh sets the tone for fairness and connection—new arrangements sealed over loaves, quarrels set aside as the growing season wanes. No two gatherings look quite the same, but each carries echoes of ancient patterns, where joining together in play and feasting honors both the land's bounty and the responsibilities that come with it (ipsadmin, 2024).

Across centuries, people have stretched and reworked these festivals to meet changing needs. Modern Pagans might celebrate with public holidays or new kinds of community events, while some families quietly mark the days with homemade crafts or favorite meals. Traditions cross lines—sometimes blending with Christian rites or local habits—and that is part of their living strength. What matters most is showing care, asking questions, and respecting the festival's meaning for others.

Next, we'll step beyond the four cornerstones of the year and trace how the movements of sun and stars helped shape calendars and guide seasonal observance, drawing the wider horizon closer for all who watched the sky (ipsadmin, 2024).

Solstices and Equinoxes

Between the dramatic fire festivals, communities also watched the sun's path, reading solstices and equinoxes as signals for sowing, harvest, and passage. These turning points in the solar year—the longest and shortest days, balanced by moments when day and night matched—brought their own quiet sense of pause to folk calendars. Unlike the bustling gatherings at Samhain or Beltane, these solar events often unfolded in ways both subtle and splendid, marked less by bonfire and feast than by careful observation of the light and its effects on field, house, and body.

The engineering of certain ancient monuments made sunlight visible and meaningful on these days. At Newgrange in Ireland, by midwinter, dawn's first rays pour through a narrow passage, flooding the burial chamber with gold light. This yearly spectacle is no accident. Builders shaped stone and space so that only at winter solstice would light reach its heart—a vivid reminder to dark-season communities that spring would return. On Scotland's Isle of Lewis, the Callanish stones stand in patterns that pick out midsummer sunrise and sunset. When summer solstice comes, shadows stretch across the ring's worn grass, marking time in a language older than story.

These alignments did more than impress; they offered shared clocks before the pocket-watch existed. A household could look to the local cairn or standing stone and know the season had turned. Such solar markers blended seamlessly with household routines: seed was blessed after seeing the first shaft of solstice light, herds moved when the sun reached a certain angle behind the hills, and prayers for rain or warmth were timed to the calendar inscribed by sky and stone. Later Christian tradition often layered new stories atop old places—dedicating wells to saints or linking mountains to miracles—

Chapter 4: The Turning Year: Seasonal Rhythms and Folk Calendars

but rarely erased this solar foundation (Campbell, 2025). The sun's track in the land remained practical and spiritual alike, shaping the rhythm of village and field.

For most families, decisions about working the land paid close attention to daylight. After the equinox, when hours of light grew or shrank rapidly, timing became crucial. Spring's equal balance told folk to watch for thawing earth and sprouting greens. When summer's days stretched long, people used the extra light for haymaking, repairing tools, and storing up against coming storms. Actual work, though, followed soil and weather. Fields weren't sown just because the sun stood high; readiness meant checking grain for hardness, feeling if the grass cured well in the air, or squeezing soil to test moisture. Festivals clustered where the labor window allowed fairs, markets, and big tasks while roads and seas were open. Solar dates were helpful guides, but they worked best alongside sharp eyes and patient hands.

Beyond the monuments and official calendars, ordinary folks read the sun and stars almost every day. Old proverbs like "A wet and windy May fills the barn with corn and hay" condensed years of watching clouds, winds, and sky-colors into reminders that guided choices. Red sunsets promised fair weather, while halos around the moon warned of rain, signaling when it was wise to hurry with hay or fish. In late summer, the appearance of the Pleiades star cluster signaled the last safe moment for gathering crops before autumn rains. Fisherfolk along coasts watched lunar phases to judge tides, knowing spring high tides brought seaweed—or risks—for boats and nets. Birds flying low before rain, sudden mists after hot days, and the way dew formed all shaped daily rhythms, blending solar knowledge with lived observation (Campbell, 2025).

Clerical records added another layer of timekeeping that echoed community needs. Monasteries tracked the date of Easter by calculating the spring equinox and full moon, but annals also noted storms, crop failures, animal migrations, and unusual happenings in the weather. Holy days like Rogationtide brought blessings to fields and processions through planted land, joining sacred calendars with farming's demands. Scribes wrote by candlelight about eclipses and celestial events, but they didn't overlook hardships caused by a cold summer or failed harvest—these accounts give modern readers windows into how natural cycles and spiritual observance wove together year by year. The church's record-keeping preserved memories not just of saints and princes but of everyday survival, showing the real impact of solstices, equinoxes, and the changing sky (Campbell, 2025).

These solar cues worked hand-in-hand with on-the-ground signs—migrating birds, budding plants, and tidal rhythms—that we'll explore next. With the sky's pacing established, attention turned to the ground, where ordinary people read the season in the unfolding life around them.

Chapter 4: The Turning Year: Seasonal Rhythms and Folk Calendars

Work, Weather, and Wonder

Beyond these formal markers like stone circles or abbey calendars, life in rural Celtic lands found its rhythm in the living world's patterns. Swallows returning over the fields, new calls from curlews in the bogs, blossoms on blackthorn hedges—all served as reminders and signals for work and celebration. While solar events gave a broad outline of the year, daily survival often depended more on watching what nature was doing right then. Farmers and fishers did not just follow dates—they read signs that told them when to sow barley, move cattle, or risk a journey across swollen rivers.

In every valley and glen, people became natural phenologists before anyone knew the word. Phenology means observing when plants bloom or birds arrive—watching for changes that announce shifts in season. The first sighting of a swallow circling near the barn often signaled soil was finally warming enough to plant oats. A chorus of curlew calls rose up ahead of rain, giving shepherds warning to bring flocks closer before wet weather made hillsides treacherous. Blossoms told their own story: blackthorn's froth of white flowers marked weeks when late frost could still strike hard, the so-called 'blackthorn winter.' Only when hawthorn followed with its sweeter scent and creamy petals did planting feel safe. These weren't superstitions but memory carried through years—one person's cold snap becoming next generation's warning. Bee activity around blooming gorse or heather revealed more than nectar flow; bees flying low meant rain was coming, while busy hives around gorse hinted at a good spell for gathering turf or hay. Observation fed family health and fortune, passed quietly between neighbors and kin.

On the coast, knowledge gathered through tides and winds shaped every choice. Lunar phases ruled fishing plans as much as church feast days did. New and full moons pulled spring tides—stronger surges that left rocky reefs bare and sent shoals crowding shallows. A neap tide, gentler and more predictable, gave safer footing for mending nets or digging shellfish. Fishers timed journeys by wind as much as moon: an east wind chilled the sea and drove mackerel away, while a steady southwesterly brought milder air and drew herring shoals close. Some families kept notes scratched into slate or old journals, recording which coves built up sand after gales, which headlands caught sudden squalls, and when certain fish returned. In many villages, everyone—from elders to children—shared in this memory. It anchored safety at sea and helped protect precious resources. Such care in tracking the elements meant fewer lost boats, better harvests, and a sense of stewardship rooted in practice rather than rulebooks (*Word Filter*, 2025).

Proverbs condensed all this learning into lines easy to remember and share. Rhymes like 'A wet and windy May fills the barn with corn and hay' carried meaning far beyond simple weather talk. They captured experience: damp and storm in early summer fed growing crops, promising plenty for the following months. Rhyme turned observation into teaching

Chapter 4: The Turning Year: Seasonal Rhythms and Folk Calendars

tool. For communities where few read and most worked alongside children, proverbs were portable wisdom—tools as useful as any sickle or spade. Travelers recalled which roads flooded by repeating sayings they'd learned at home, or warned others of shifting winds while out in the fields. Proverbs changed from place to place, with different lines for valleys or uplands. This flexibility respected microclimates, encouraging each community to value the evidence right outside their door instead of relying on distant rules or 'official' calendars. Folk wisdom remained democratic, open to testing and change, inviting even outsiders to listen closely and learn what counted as true in each landscape.

Local landscapes created exceptions that were just as important as patterns shared across the islands. Uplands held frost long after primroses peeped from lowland meadows, forcing herders to wait before moving flocks or planting beans. Atlantic fog crept inland, delaying blossom on coastal apple trees and throwing off orchard timelines set by textbooks. Sea winds dried laundry quickly some years but soaked it for weeks in others, prompting families to shift festival dates or market days by intuition rather than calculation. Community tradition was never static. Folk calendars flexed with each year's surprises, adapting to microclimates that could change within a half-day's walk. When customs shifted by a week or two, it was not loss but wisdom—an understanding that survival and celebration both thrive when people honor the reality of their own places. What may seem like magical insight is, in truth, careful attention passed down, honed by need and woven into daily life. This practice of noticing prepares us for seeing our own surroundings anew, as the next section will help you explore through your own journal.

Reflecting with the Year

Historical communities relied closely on careful observation of land, weather, and sky. They watched for signs—from the flowering of elder along an Irish hedgerow to the shift in sheep's coats ahead of a Highland frost—to guide their work and ritual. While these details meant survival and timing for them, you have space to make this attentiveness a grounding practice. You do not need to replicate their lives; your rhythms can honor theirs through steady attention to the seasons where you live.

Set a Year Wheel

The year wheel offers a creative way to track time's turning. Start with a circle divided into twelve sections—one for each month. Around the rim, add your own touch: local holidays, family gatherings, first or last frost, full moons, or any event that resonates. This is your tool, so there are no required labels. Pick two or three themes that matter and assign each a color or symbol. Perhaps you follow changes in birdlife, the taste of air before rain, or when neighborhood gardens burst into bloom. Someone near the Cornish coast might mark foggy

Chapter 4: The Turning Year: Seasonal Rhythms and Folk Calendars

mornings and fishing boat returns, while city dwellers could follow street tree leaves or shifts in market produce. Leave some extra margin for noting outlying moments—a sudden hailstorm in March, strawberries ripening early, or a festival date moving. These "anomalies" help show how every cycle has its surprises. The point is not to force the year into exact patterns but to notice which weave together over time. Patterns reveal themselves slowly, often only after several cycles (lovedoesthat, 2024).

Weekly Field Walks

Pick one loop you can visit without much planning—a path around an apartment block, a woodland edge, or a walk past community allotments. Commit to walking it once a week, aiming for a similar day or time. Each outing, jot down three sensory details: a robin's song echoing across wet stone, the smell of cut grass, puddles freezing hard overnight, the sharpness of wind by late October. Snap a quick photo, draw a small sketch, or record a voice memo if writing feels heavy. The aim is to witness change as it happens. Honest noticing beats perfect knowledge: if you don't know the name of the yellow flower by the park bench, just describe its shape or color.

Ethical care sits at the heart of Celtic folkways. Stay on marked paths so roots and moss beds stay undisturbed. Watch birds and wild creatures from a distance. Do not pick plants or handle nests. If your walk brings you near a churchyard, well, or sacred grove, treat these places quietly. Refrain from taking photos of people, moving offerings, or sharing exact locations online. These boundaries show respect both to place and to community, echoing reciprocity's lessons from earlier chapters (lovedoesthat, 2024). Missed weeks don't break the practice—return when you're able, and let the habit flex with life's turns (lovedoesthat, 2024).

Household Markers

Home life mirrors the seasons, even if you live in an upstairs flat in the center of town. Track what shifts as months pass— do you switch from soups to salads as days grow longer? When does your energy lean toward cleaning, decluttering, or making something new? Notice when berries or fresh greens appear at the market, if preserves run low on the shelf by winter's end, or if heating bills rise with the cold. Maybe you start knitting again when evenings turn dark or take up sketching outside as soon as snow melts in the glen. None of these changes are mystical—they are answers to daylight, warmth, hunger, and mood. Record them without judgment; your household pattern may have little in common with those who timed chores to sheep-shearing or grain-threshing. That's part of honoring your context as one thread in the broader fabric.

Chapter 4: The Turning Year: Seasonal Rhythms and Folk Calendars

End-of-Season Review

Toward the end of each season, pause to look back. Take half an hour with your year wheel, field walk notes, and home observations. What keeps showing up? Which events stand alone, never quite repeating? Maybe you find that apples peak later than you expected or that coastal storms always cluster in early November. Write a short journal entry covering what you noticed, what caught you off guard, and what seems worth watching next year. Ask yourself what might have shaped your data—a weeklong flu, noisy roadwork, or travel could all influence what you saw or missed.

This review isn't about producing a perfect record—it's about building relationship and clarity. Note repeatable trends, but be wary of drawing big conclusions from one odd occurrence. As a gentle next step, name one action for the coming season: buy fruit at a local stall, try planting native herbs on your balcony, look up the story behind a local hill, or offer volunteer hands for park care. These gestures return attention and respect to the land, echoing age-old habits of reciprocity and thanks (lovedoesthat, 2024). Next year, another layer adds to your understanding, and the slow revealing of pattern continues, just as it did for those who came before.

Bringing It All Together

Looking back at the traditions explored in this chapter, it's clear that timekeeping in the Celtic world was never just about marking dates on a calendar. People tuned their lives to the steady pulse of fire festivals and the subtle turning points of sun and season. These practices were woven with memory, gratitude, and community care—tools for facing uncertainty and celebrating what mattered. From lighting protective fires at Samhain to watching the sky for solstice dawn, every act was both practical and heartfelt. This layered approach invited everyone—not just leaders or experts—to take part in shaping and remembering the year together.

The folk wisdom handed down through generations encourages us to pay attention and find meaning in our own surroundings. Whether tracking birds, seasons, or the small changes in daily life, the spirit of these old customs still fits in a modern world when we make space for mindful noticing. Time can be measured by more than numbers—it's found in shared meals, seasonal routines, and quiet acts of care. By stepping into this tradition of observation, you join a line of people who honored land and community with every choice. The invitation is simple: slow down, look closely, and let your own story find its rhythm within the cycles that have shaped so many lives before ours.

Chapter 5: Plants as Teachers: Trees, Herbs, and Hedgerow Wisdom

In the quiet corners of history, certain plants stand out not just for their physical presence but for the roles they played in shaping daily lives. Imagine a 19th-century road crew in western Ireland who chose to divert an entire lane simply to avoid disturbing a solitary hawthorn known as the May Bush. This wasn't just a tree; it was a marker of community respect and tradition. Years later, villagers from the same area would tie ribbons to its branches every spring, hoping for luck at the cattle market. Meanwhile, across the sea in a Highland glen, a herdsman's words from the 1930s tell us about crossing a rowan twig with red thread over his byre door after a neighbor's cow fell ill—a small act of care and protection. And nearby, an ancient oak stood firm as the village meeting place, earning the name "Assembly Tree" on maps and in local memory. Over in Brittany, families gathered beneath yews each year to honor those who had passed, believing the evergreen's steadiness helped keep memories alive through harsh winters. These stories offer glimpses into how plants weren't merely background scenery but central to law, protection, and remembrance in communities' everyday rhythms.

Looking closely at these snapshots reveals deep roots in the meanings held by sacred trees and plants—meanings that shaped how people interacted with the land and one another. From boundary guardians like the hawthorn, to the strong oaks under which decisions were made, the protective rowans hung at thresholds, and the yews connecting generations through time, each plant carried lessons in presence and respect. This chapter invites you to explore those connections, uncovering the wisdom embedded in trees, herbs, and hedgerow life. It encourages a way of learning that listens carefully, honors traditions, and embraces the living relationships between people and the plants that have quietly taught them for centuries.

Sacred Trees in Context

Living near the same trees day after day, Celtic communities saw them not as materials to be used but as neighbors—beings with memory and presence. This relational way of seeing sets the foundation for interacting with plants in folk practice, echoing what we explored about connectedness and reciprocity with the land itself in Chapter 3. The meaning of a tree came from how people lived alongside it: walking past the hawthorn at the edge of the field, gathering beneath the old oak, leaving ribbons on the rowan, or pausing under the yew in winter. Trees marked boundaries, welcomed gatherings, offered protection, and held memories that tied generations to place (*The Guardian Trees of Ireland | Irish Folkore from the Emerald Isle*, n.d.).

Hawthorn as Boundary Guardian

Hawthorn's dense thorns and sudden white blossoms make it an unmistakable marker in fields, along roads, and at the edges of villages. Across western Ireland and Highland Scotland, lone hawthorns stood at crossroads, wells, and property lines—living signals of transition and protection. Road crews sometimes bent their work around these trees instead of disturbing them. In May, when hawthorn bursts into flower, communities carried out the May Bush tradition: ribbons, bits of cloth, or colored eggshells were tied onto branches outside homes, expressing wishes for safe passage through the threshold into summer. These actions weren't based on distant symbolism but on the close knowledge that boundaries are fragile and need guardians. Taboo against cutting or moving these trees was real and enforced by custom; even today, stories abound of misfortune following the careless removal of a boundary hawthorn. By letting the tree stand, people honored the liminal—the in-between spaces where daily life meets mystery (*The Guardian Trees of Ireland | Irish Folkore from the Emerald Isle*, n.d.).

Oak as Symbol of Strength and Law

Place-names across Ireland—like Doire, Derrynane, Derrybeg—mark where oaks once grew and where assemblies met under their shelter. Oaks served as natural roofs and reliable landmarks for gathering, making decisions, and resolving disputes. Their strong wood built trackways over boggy ground and supported the crannógs—lake dwellings that needed foundations able to stand the test of time (*The Guardian Trees of Ireland | Irish Folkore from the Emerald Isle*, n.d.). When oaths were sworn beneath the spreading branches, the steadfastness of the oak became part of the community's fabric. Oak bonfires at communal festivals did more than give warmth; they represented endurance and continuity, not because of magical attributes but because these trees had always been part of such events. As with the hawthorn, patterns seen at the level of village assembly—gathering under oaks, trusting in their protection—also appeared at thresholds, such as hanging rowan by the door, showing how tree relationships shaped both public and private life.

Rowan as Protective Ward

Rowan's slender trunk, feathered leaves, and bright red berries made it easy to spot and easy to remember. Folklore held that the red color kept away trouble, signaling alertness

Chapter 5: Plants as Teachers: Trees, Herbs, and Hedgerow Wisdom

and defense. In the Highlands, people threaded pieces of red yarn through rowan twigs to form small crosses, which they then hung over byre doors or tucked into travelers' packs. These tokens weren't just about superstition—they mirrored practical awareness that danger lurked at meeting-places: house thresholds, animal shelters, paths out onto the moor. Burning rowan casually was frowned upon, recognizing its special status as a ward against ill will. Communities believed rowan sharpened "second sight," meaning clear-seeing—not so much prophecy, but the practical gift of perceiving threats before they arrived. Stories collected from Highland elders describe rowan trees left to grow beside wells, guarding places where water and land meet, and tokens kept close during times of uncertainty. This role was entirely rooted in repeated practice; every spring brought new thread, new hope (*The Guardian Trees of Ireland | Irish Folkore from the Emerald Isle*, n.d.).

Yew as Memorial and Continuity

Yew trees, with their dark evergreen needles and ancient trunks, grew in churchyards and burial grounds all across the Celtic world. Their ability to live for centuries made them living witnesses to generations of prayers, grief, and joy. Yews don't drop all their leaves in winter, so their green persists through the most barren months, turning them into quiet companions through seasons of lack and cold (*The Guardian Trees of Ireland | Irish Folkore from the Emerald Isle*, n.d.). The slow growth and poisonous seeds added gravity to their presence, reinforcing respect—people gathered beneath them to remember the dead and to mark the passing of time. Yew groves became places where patience and memory took root, where children learned about ancestors and communities felt connection to those who had gone before. Breton parishes still keep annual vigils beneath the yew, blending prayer and storytelling by candlelight. The solemn power of the yew comes not from abstract meaning but from being present at the hinge where life meets death, year after year.

Having located cultural meaning in the trees themselves, we can now turn to what it means to engage ethically with the living teachers of hedgerow and woodland—learning first with care and attention before taking any branch or leaf.

Herbal Knowledge and Care

Building on the principles of reciprocity with land introduced in Chapter 3, every step in working with herbs arises from observation and respect. Just as we learned to approach sacred places with consent and care, living plant communities call for the same attention—rooted in curiosity, not assumption. Before touching a leaf or gathering a sprig, pause to watch what thrives here: Is the ground sun-soaked or shaded? Does soil squish underfoot, hinting at a wet meadow, or crunch with the heather of upland heath? Wet meadow plants, like meadowsweet or marsh marigold, often cluster where water pools, their feet damp and roots tangled among

Chapter 5: Plants as Teachers: Trees, Herbs, and Hedgerow Wisdom

mosses. By contrast, herbs like ling and bell heather signal open, breezy ground where soil drains fast and gorse holds back wind. Reading habitat means looking not just for one plant, but noticing the mosaic—companion planting in nature tells whether a spot welcomes gathering or needs to be left alone (Ellis, 1994).

Researching local conservation status is an act of respect and responsibility. Trusted sources such as the National Biodiversity Data Centre (Ireland), Botanical Society of Britain & Ireland, or your regional wildlife trust provide up-to-date lists on protected or endangered species. If a plant appears on these lists or looks rare, it's off-limits for harvest: observing and learning becomes your practice here, protecting both scarcity and your own safety. Only abundant, thriving stands belong in a gatherer's basket—and even then, the roots should remain untouched, as uprooting breaks more than earth; it severs connections for seasons to come.

Consent goes beyond personal intention—land has boundaries, and so do those who steward it. Always seek permission before entering private land, whether by knocking at a cottage door or sending a message to a landowner. A simple, honest approach—"Hello, I'm learning about local herbs and wonder if you'd allow me to observe plants in your hedgerow"—opens doors respectfully. Where open-access traditions exist, like Scotland's right-to-roam, welcome is balanced by codes of conduct: close gates behind you, stick to footpaths when possible, and avoid trampling sensitive areas. Public land rarely means unlimited use; each place carries its own expectations shaped by history and custom (Ó Giolláin, 2000).

Botanical safety starts with careful identification. Never rely on a single feature; look at leaf shape, the way stems feel, flower color, scent, and when a plant blooms. Familiarize yourself with dangerous twins—hemlock mimics wild carrot, while foxglove sometimes hides among comfrey. Learning these differences is empowering, turning risk into a chance to slow down and notice deeply. Use gloves and clean snips, not bare hands or rough pulls. If there's any doubt about identity, let questions hold your hand back—uncertainty is a prompt to learn, not a sign of failure. Safe practice protects everyone—yourself, the plants, and those who share these spaces after you.

Approaching harvest as relationship-building brings to life the ethics explored further in Chapter 9. The "one-in-twenty" guideline asks that only a small fraction of healthy populations be gathered. This leaves most of the stand to flower, fruit, feed insects, and return seed to soil. Kneel gently to avoid crushing roots, cut cleanly above the base, and move with care to leave little trace beyond gratitude. Signs of stress—wilting, patchy growth, bite marks from grazing animals—mean stepping back. Instead of taking, give back by picking litter, reporting invasive species, or making sure fences and gates are secure. In this, gratitude becomes a gesture that matches or outweighs what is received (MacNeill, 1951).

Plant knowledge is always tied to people and places. Passing along a charm or herbal recipe calls for naming where it comes from—Irish, Scottish, Welsh, or Breton custom—along with the language and whether it lives in oral memory or written tradition. When quoting living elders or herbalists, ask permission and be generous with credit or thanks. Living cultures are not resources to borrow without limit, but neighbors with boundaries and wishes. Respectful attribution might sound like, "This recipe comes from a Welsh-speaking family in Gwynedd, shared with their blessing," while an uncredited tale erases real histories. Embracing this diversity honors the many voices that shape Celtic herbal traditions, inviting readers to listen as much as they learn (Uí Choncheanainn, 1987).

With these ethical foundations in place, we can better appreciate how plants appeared in everyday protective and blessing lore—not as instructions to copy, but as cultural expressions rooted in relationship. Understanding these relationships helps us move with care into the household charms that follow, carrying forward both safety and respect.

Household Plant Charms

With an ethical lens now in place—one shaped by care, safety, and reciprocity—stories of household plant charms become something richer than simple superstition. These practices appear in memory as reflections of neighborly protection, trust between land and people, and the hope that right relationship could ripple through every room. In Highland crofts and island cottages, rowan stood watch at doors and paths, not as a vague magical tool but as a marker: this household belongs to itself. Accounts describe rowan twigs tucked above lintels or tied with red thread on key hooks—a signal both practical and symbolic. The red, seen across Indo-European traditions as a barrier against harm, gleamed bright against stone or peat, announcing that luck was welcome and misfortune denied entry. Ritual timing—for instance, just before birthing seasons or spring festivals—gave these gestures their rhythm in daily life. Placing new branches after winter or when calves arrived offered fresh beginnings, entwining household routine with cycles of growth and renewal (Electric Witch, 2025).

Stories tell of other doorways filled with the scent of juniper. Barn saining—sometimes remembered as a slow smolder, sometimes as a full smoke bath—took shape each year before cattle went out to pasture. Elders recall beds of embers laid with juniper sprigs, filling byres and halls with blue-grey haze until even the beams were sweetened. Then, windows and doors swung wide, letting in clear air and sending away all that was stale. These stories center on careful intention: too much smoke could harm as easily as help, so the act bridged caution with communal well-being. Barns, homes, and herds shared the cleansing together. Saining happened not from rote habit but as recognition of seasonal shifts—the work of opening and closing, waiting and releasing, all within a small circle of kin.

Accounts from Irish, Scottish, and Breton communities hold vivid images of St. John's wort gathered for midsummer. On St. John's Eve, folk would seek the plant as the sun set, gathering bright clusters while voices carried across fields. Back home,

Chapter 5: Plants as Teachers: Trees, Herbs, and Hedgerow Wisdom

sprigs found their places in rafters, woven into window frames, slipped behind bedposts, or pressed between pages of worn family Bibles. Over weeks, the plant's condition served as a quiet oracle: thriving leaves spoke of good fortune ahead, while blackening stems signaled caution. Young people might tuck sprigs under pillows to dream of future love, or leave them by shoes to ask about safe passage. Variations flowed from region to region—bundles tied with colored yarn, dried stalks set above hearthstones—but each practice reflected hopes for luck, insight, and healing carried on the breath of summer nights.

Every February brought households together to weave Brigid's crosses from rushes cut by local streambanks. Grandmothers taught nimble-fingered children how to turn green blades over one another by lamplight, binding them tight at the heart and loose at the ends. Old hands knew which meadows gave the best rushes, so this custom drew families out, reminding them that blessing always began outside with bare feet in cool grass. When finished, each cross hung above doors, near kitchen stoves, or up on rafters, where it would stay for a whole turning of the year. With the next Imbolc, last year's cross moved gently to the fire, and a new one took its place. The act marked both continuity and change—house and land renewing their promises. Stories lingered long after: a cross fallen early prompted gentle worry, a rush pulled from the thatch became a lucky token for travelers, and silence around the hearth grew soft and expectant on winter's rim.

The details of these practices shifted with landscape, season, and the hands that shaped them. No single gesture can stand alone; meaning rises from the full pattern—who gathers the rush, who sweeps the hearth, what time of night the doorway is crossed. In each telling, plants offer more than mere defense or luck. They become teachers threaded through everyday life, rooting presence and belonging in tangible acts. These practices point us toward attentive observation rather than imitation. Having seen how plants held meaning in context, we can now listen to our own local hedgerows, inviting them to reveal themselves through quiet, thoughtful presence— moving gently from cultural story to personal connection (Electric Witch, 2025).

Learning from the Hedgerow

Household plant customs like rowan charms, juniper smoke cleansing, and St. John's wort hanging share something quietly profound—the power of attention to place, timing, and relationship. These traditions connect people to home ground through familiar gestures and objects, rooted in land, season, and story. Rather than trying to copy these practices detail for detail, you can honor their spirit by learning directly from living plants nearby, meeting them with presence and care instead of aiming to collect or claim.

A hedgerow, field edge, or even a park border makes a perfect outdoor classroom for this kind of learning. Before setting out, tuck a notebook, pencil, gloves, and a small bag into your pocket—tools for noticing rather than taking. When you

Chapter 5: Plants as Teachers: Trees, Herbs, and Hedgerow Wisdom

arrive, try a five-senses walk. Brush fingertips over bark: feel the silkiness of birch, the deep grooves of oak, the waxy shine of holly leaves, or the softness of young nettles (with care). Lean in to catch how leaves smell on a sun-warmed afternoon, or after rain has passed. Listen to the different hushes and rattles as wind moves through hawthorn, bramble, or beech. Taste stays out of bounds here—no nibbling—but let your eyes drink in every color, pattern, and flicker of movement along the tangled green edge. Pause at boundary places where one habitat meets another, watching which plants gather at crossings of light and shadow, damp and dry. This is not about taking samples, but letting each sense guide you toward questions and wonder. Leaving with empty hands sets a gentle rule: what matters most is noticing and remembering, not owning or using. You may find that what you bring home in notes and memory roots more deeply than any gathered sprig ever could (Long et al., 2025).

Sketching acts as its own silent teacher. A quick drawing—a leaf's outline, the twist of a stem, the shadows cast by yew needles—is less about art and more about honest seeing. Are the leaves rough-edged or smooth? Do they grow opposite each other or take turns up the stalk? Noticing how many veins run through a leaf or which plants crowd its feet draws your mind deeper into quiet observation. Next to each drawing, jot down where you found it: Was the ground damp, the shade thick, or sunlight patchy? Who are its neighbors—honeysuckle winding up a fence, ivy draping over a stone, bramble weaving through hazel? These notes teach you how plant communities hold together, telling their own stories about moisture, shelter, and belonging. Resist the urge to look things up right away. Instead, fill your pages with slow drawings and questions. Only when you're back indoors, with time to consider and compare, reach for a field guide. Matching leaf edges and stems at home lets patience do its work, preventing rushed mistakes and giving you space to meet each plant on its terms (Long et al., 2025).

Honoring the ways plants are known locally builds both humility and connection. Wild chervil might have a dozen names within twenty miles, and each holds a slice of history, language, or ritual. If someone offers you a local name—maybe an elder calls bramble by its Irish, Scots, or Welsh word—treat it with care. Ask gently how to spell or say it, and see if there's a story behind the name. Remember this knowledge is shared, not owed, and always ask before repeating a tale or writing down what someone tells you by name. Some plant wisdom lives within families or neighborhoods, kept close for good reason. Saying, "May I share what you've told me?" honors these boundaries, teaching that respect runs as deep as curiosity. In your notes, record both the folk name and the Latin; holding both reminds you every plant carries more than one identity—scientific, cultural, and personal—all worth recognizing thoughtfully.

Reciprocity goes beyond restraint—it means caring for the places that welcome your footsteps. Bringing gloves and a small bag signals readiness to leave the hedgerow lighter than you found it. Picking up cans, bottles, or plastic wrappers becomes a simple offering to the land. Stick to gathering only human litter, staying clear of nests, burrows, and undisturbed moss. Step around tender seedlings and steer boots wide of wildflowers pushing up between thorns. If you stumble on dumped rubbish, invasive growth overtaking native plants, or signs of bigger harm, note them and alert local authorities or conservation groups so solutions come from those equipped for the job. Each return can close with a moment of gratitude—closing a farm gate firmly, brushing dirt off your boots before leaving delicate grass, and pausing to notice the way sunset slips over leaves. These actions make each visit accountable and caring, setting a model for how to meet all forms of ancestral knowledge—with humility, patience, and open-eyed attention (Long et al., 2025).

Bringing It All Together

Looking back at the stories and traditions we've explored, it's clear that sacred trees were far more than silent symbols in Celtic landscapes. Each plant—hawthorn, oak, rowan, yew—was woven into the fabric of daily life, guiding protection, marking boundaries, nurturing memory, and rooting communities to place and season. The details might shift from village to valley or from one family's telling to another, but the pattern remains: meaning grew from lived relationship. Whether tying ribbons for luck or leaving a cross above the doorway, these acts carried wishes for safety, belonging, and care through good years and hard ones alike.

All of this invites us to slow down and look closely at the world outside our own doors. Instead of seeking out exact replicas of old customs, we can honor their spirit by listening to the plants that share our spaces today—meeting them with attention, curiosity, and respect. The lessons of the hawthorn or yew aren't locked away in distant folklore; they're alive in the ways we move gently, seek permission, notice changes, and give back to the land. Building real connection always begins with presence and thoughtful practice, opening a path for tradition to grow in new soil while honoring its roots.

Chapter 6: Stones, Water, and Weather: Elemental Kinships

On a windswept hillside, your phone buzzes with an alert: a gale is coming. Meanwhile, just over the ridge, an elder tilts their head to the sky, eyes tracing the thin, wispy mare's-tail clouds stretching across a dull gray ceiling, predicting that same storm before any device could. Nearby, a pilgrim carefully threads a ribbon onto the branches of a hawthorn beside a well said to hold healing waters, while a group of hikers tracks a carved boundary stone on their GPS screens a mile away. These moments, though separated by time and technology, share a common thread: each person seeks their way in the world, protective signs, and confirmation that they belong within the land's story.

These acts of care and connection invite us to consider how stones, waters, and skies have held stories, warnings, and meaning for generations in Celtic places. From the quiet steadfastness of standing stones marking boundaries to the flowing rituals around holy wells, and the living wisdom found in reading the weather above, this chapter unfolds how elemental kinships shaped community life and memory. We'll journey through these ancient markers and meanings to understand why they still echo deeply today, offering guidance and grounding in a changing world.

Standing Stones and Carved Marks

On a day when our phones and watches run out of charge, it's easy to forget that once, orientation began with stones. There were no screens to tell people where they stood or what they owned—only the enduring presence of rock in field and valley. Imagine walking along grassy lanes and coming upon a lump of granite rising out of turf: here, the boundary of your parish is not an invisible line but a boulder every neighbor knows. That stone means grazing rights end here, and another family's flock begins. In scattered settlements, these markers were as dependable as any map, anchoring people to place even when seasons blurred paths and borders.

Some stones took on names and fame: "the Treaty Stone," "the Fair Stone," or other titles local tongues gave them. These became meeting points for annual markets, marriage arrangements, and fair judgments. You might picture a cluster gathered on a chilly morning, huddled around a broad stone slab while bargains and grievances played out within earshot of the silent witness. The stone itself held the memory. When deals were struck, the landscape was the record-keeper, ensuring public agreements could not be quietly undone (Ó Giolláin, 2000). In this way, standing stones worked like a community bulletin board made of granite—public, fixed, and, above all, reliable.

Chapter 6: Stones, Water, and Weather: Elemental Kinships

Writing arrived at these stones in the form of Ogham—an alphabet of lines carved into the edges of upright slabs. Ogham wasn't just graffiti; it was a way of rooting memory in place. Names, kin groups, and sometimes simple messages declared, "This person belonged here; this story happened here." Seeing your ancestor inscribed along the stone meant knowing you were tethered by more than words—you were part of the landscape itself (McManus, 1991). Later on, Christian crosses appeared, sometimes chiseled onto much older stones. Rather than erasing the past, these new marks layered over the old, creating what scholars call a palimpsest—a manuscript written over again, yet still bearing faint traces of earlier tales. Each mark added another chapter, not by discarding what came before but by folding new meanings into stone's surface (Crawford, 1926). Churches and chapels often built walls with such marked boulders, blending old reverence with new faith in a conversation that never quite ended.

Walking past these stones, travelers wove small gestures into their routines. A pin tucked into a crevice, a coin dropped beside roots, a rag tied to a bush nearby—each acted as a greeting to the place. As we explored in Chapter 3, offerings mark reciprocal relationships rather than transactions. Leaving something at the stone wasn't about buying favor but acknowledging presence—an unspoken exchange between person and place. You might pause at a healing stone with a pin if you needed luck, or whisper a wish at a marker known for safe passage. This practice shifted from hill to hill; one village left ribbons, another swore by smooth pebbles. What you offered depended on the stories tied to that particular stone. No single formula governed these acts. Instead, each gesture grew from local practice and remembered tales, reinforcing that folk magic is a language learned from the land, not imposed upon it (Evans, 1957). These practices raise questions about respectful engagement we'll address more fully when we consider contemporary ethics in Chapter 9, since many stones remain meaningful to living communities today.

Distinctive stones draw stories as surely as they mark boundaries. An erratic left by the last ice age, a huge rock split by frost, or a hollowed stone filled by rainwater often became magnets for tale-telling. People said a giant tossed the stone across the valley in a fit of temper, or a saint knelt there so long her knees wore hollows in the granite. Sometimes these stories explained the strange shapes, but they also taught values: respect for borders, the price of broken promises, courage in hard times. Children learned both landscape and lore by tracing the parish edge from stone to stone: "That's the Giant's Chair, just before the turn to the oak grove." Here, geography stuck in memory because story and rock were inseparable. These narratives did more than amuse—they taught ways to live in place, making moral lessons as visible as the boulders that inspired them. Storytelling at these sites was less about superstition than education, using terrain as the world's oldest mnemonic device (Ó Giolláin, 2000).

Stones endure. They answer the need for shared memory, boundary, and witness in a way that oral tradition alone cannot. Unlike wooden posts weathering away or rumors shifting with each retelling, a stone remains to say: this agreement, this story, this relationship holds. While stones stood as witnesses to agreements and boundaries, waters invited a different kind of relationship—one measured in circuits, prayers, and offerings that moved with the seasons.

Holy Wells and Springs

Just as standing stones mark the land with enduring memory, holy wells and springs draw people into a living relationship with place through flow, return, and ritual care. Where stone offers solidity and witness, water entices with movement and the promise of change. At a pattern day—a local festival honoring a holy well—friends and strangers arrive at dawn or under an open sky, drawn by shared rhythm. The path to the well winds through dew-wet grass. Some walk sunwise, moving clockwise as generations have before them. This direction honors both folk tradition and, in many places, pre-Christian roots, echoing the daily arc of the sun across the land. Touching the cold surface, hands dip cups and fill bottles as prayers are murmured. Water is sprinkled on foreheads, wounds, and keepsakes. Stepping through this round, each person weaves new memories into a much older tapestry, exchanging news, sharing food, and tying a living thread between body, place, and season (Borkowicz, 2025).

Pattern days are not about spectacle or magic tricks. They often fall on saints' feast days or moments marked out by seasonal change, such as February 1st for St. Brigid's wells in

Ireland. People bring bread, cheese, or home-baked cake, laying out cloths for neighbors and travelers alike. Ritual movement—circling the well three times, washing eyes or hands—blends with quiet moments: the slow kneeling, the hush of hope or gratitude. Sometimes, healing is sought for a friend; at other times, water is carried home to a relative who could not attend. These acts build community memory, shaping a sense of belonging to each other and to the landscape.

Next to many wells grows a tree called a cloutie bush. Tradition invites visitors to tie a small strip of natural cloth—a cloutie—to a branch as they whisper a wish or prayer. As the cloth weathers, dissolves, or falls, it carries that intention away. In some places, every branch flutters with rags and ribbons, but deep respect guides true offering. Leaving plastic, synthetic, or brightly dyed ribbon does harm, marring beauty and risking harm to birds and animals. Cotton, linen, or wool— left only where custom welcomes them—keep the act gentle, present, and safe. If unsure, a simple pause to ask or observe teaches more than any folk handbook. Choosing unbleached cotton over a shiny gift ribbon, or even holding back altogether, honors both tradition and the well itself (Borkowicz, 2025).

Holy wells rarely belong to one era alone. Christian saints, like Brigid in Ireland or Winifred in Wales, are woven into the story, their feast days celebrated with processions, candlelight, and shared song. Some wells carry tales of miracle cures—an injured child healed after a mother's prayer, or a weary traveler revived by a cup of water. These stories coexist with older customs, layering reverence rather than replacing it. At St. Winifred's Well in Wales, pilgrims once slept beside the waters, lighting candles and singing into the night. Today, families still gather around the same springs, blending new hopes with well-aged faith. Each locality brings its flavor: a picnic here, a silent vigil there, always shaped by who tends the place now as much as by what came before (Borkowicz, 2025).

Water holds presence not just for healing but as a site of truth-telling. Folklore tells of oaths sworn at wells, disputes settled by the water's edge, and vows made with the spring as witness. In some villages, neighbors would gather by torchlight if a quarrel ran deep. Words spoken within earshot of running water bound a person's honor, and in certain tales, the well itself was said to reveal falsehood—clouding the surface or refusing to be drawn. One old story describes two neighbors locked in disagreement, standing up to their knees in a chilly stream, surrounded by elders and children. The power of these rituals lay not in supernatural claims, but in the shared values of fairness and community accountability (Borkowicz, 2025).

Each of these customs reminds readers that engagement with holy wells isn't about extracting blessings or collecting stories, but about relationship and responsibility. The best way to approach any well is with humility, curiosity, and care: asking permission, observing local guidance, tending the place when needed, and resisting the urge to leave more than memory. Pattern days may pass quietly now, but their rhythms still shape how people meet the land—with food, laughter, careful steps, and words softly offered to water. From waters that heal and bear witness, our attention turns skyward, to the wisdom found in clouds and storms, as weather lore invites us further along the elemental path (Borkowicz, 2025).

Skies, Storms, and Signs

From waters that heal and witness, we look upward to where the weather unfolds in signs both subtle and grand. Celtic communities knew that the sky was no empty arch but a restless teacher, offering safety or warning with every shift of cloud, color, and light. While stones anchor and springs sustain, the sky's messages are urgent—at times gentle as a morning haze, at others fierce as spring thunder.

To those who lived by sea and river, reading the sky was daily practice. Fishers looked for "mackerel skies," bands of fishbone-patterned cirrus clouds, as a signal that wind might soon change. These clouds form high and thin, often streaked like mares' tails, hinting at moisture and invisible fronts rolling in from the Atlantic (Gebhardt, 2024). A quickening chop on slate-gray water told of rising winds; when the horizon blurred into the sea, fishers read caution. Even the color of dawn and dusk held meaning: a gold-red sunset promised stable weather, while a red glow in the eastern morning predicted storms coming from the west. "Evening red, good weather ahead, morning red threatens rain" was more than rhyme—it was wisdom proven at the cost of wet nets and safe returns

Chapter 6: Stones, Water, and Weather: Elemental Kinships

(Gebhardt, 2024). These patterns were learned patiently, one day and storm at a time, building a store of hard-won trust in what the sky revealed.

Cloud names carry their own stories. An ostratus layer—a thick, rain-producing blanket stretching low over fields—warns of an hours-long drenching (ostratus: A combination of "Nimbus" and "Stratus", indicating a broad, rain-producing layer cloud). The sight of a cumulonimbus, towering above the hills in the late afternoon, meant lightning could break loose and send everyone seeking shelter (Cumulonimbus: A combination of "Cumulus" and "Nimbus"). Sometimes, lens-shaped lenticularis clouds hovered over mountain passes, mistaken for fairy doors or omens because of their otherworldly shape (Lenticularis: "Lens-shaped", describing the typical form, which resemble lenses or UFOs). After summer storms, mammatus clouds—soft, pouch-like bulges hanging beneath thunderheads—could be seen hanging in the orange glow, interpreted as the breath of celestial cows or as warnings for shepherds (Mammatus: Derived from "Mamma," Latin for breast, describing the pouch-like forms beneath certain clouds). Each name reflects both observed reality and imagination coloring the edge of vision.

Not all weather wisdom came from the sky itself. Animals—winged and earthbound—served as barometers and forecasters. Swallows swooping near the grass hinted rain was brewing, following insects pressed downward by heavy air (Gebhardt, 2024). Bees buzzing close to their hives warned of dampness, sensing the weight of moisture even before clouds appeared overhead. Gulls flying inland roused coastal folk to bring in their gear, just as frogs croaking louder than usual signaled a coming storm. This kind of watching did not require special tools or secret skill—just willingness to notice. Each animal sign added another voice to the chorus that built a picture of what might come next.

Legends and proverbs knit these observations into shared story. A rainbow arcing over farmland after a squall was a welcome sight, sometimes read as promise of clearing weather—or elsewhere, an omen of rain yet to come, depending on its place and hour. The optics are simple: sun shining through raindrops bends the light, releasing color. Yet the meanings carried local flavor; dawn rainbows were warnings along some coasts, while evening rainbows brought relief. In some tales, rainbows marked boundaries between worlds, sanctifying crossroads or wells where spirits moved between realms (Gebhardt, 2024). So practical forecasting walked hand in hand with myth and metaphor, keeping hearts open as well as heads wary.

Storms called for humility and respect. When thunder rumbled, families shuttered windows, put away irons, covered mirrors, and paused work with metal tools or water buckets. Some whispered prayers or psalms, others simply sat together by hearth-light until the last growl passed. These customs blended caution against fire and shock with a belief that storm-spirits or saints demanded quiet. To recognize danger and listen, rather than command or dismiss, was seen as wise. Folk denied neither science nor story; they acted with care, aware that their small actions showed reverence for forces beyond their full control (Gebhardt, 2024).

This careful watching, this blend of practical skill and wonder, invites us to consider how we might extend the same care to the places we visit. When reading sky-signs, people practiced presence, relationship, and humility—qualities just as needed in our approach to sacred landscapes today. Weather lore is less about mastery and more about meeting the world as it is, with hands ready to learn and hearts open to surprise.

Caring for Sacred Places Today

Having explored how Celtic communities interpreted stones, waters, and weather as active participants in daily life, you're now ready to carry this wisdom into your own visits and practices. Now that you see how standing stones marked memory, holy wells gave healing, and skies forecasted more than rain, the next step is caring for these places so their stories continue. Modern spiritual seekers add to these traditions by the way we show respect and protection for sacred sites.

Stay on Paths: Protecting Ancient Grounds

When you stay on designated trails, you participate in long-term site preservation. Lichen grows at a pace hard to notice—a patch on an old stone may have taken decades or even centuries to form. Soil along the edge of a path compacts with every footstep; water struggles to sink in, wildflowers vanish, and roots lose air. Even one shortcut across grass becomes dozens each week, carving scars that take years to heal. Boardwalks and marked walkways aren't obstacles; they're invitations to help stones and soils outlast us all. If you visit alone or in a small group, you lower the pressure on paths, giving fragile plants and mosses more time to recover. These small acts offer a private kind of connection—more quiet, less crowd, richer moments. When you follow the boundaries set for visitors, you join hands with everyone who wants these places to thrive long after your footprint fades.

Non-Intrusive Offerings: Intention Over Objects

Sometimes a sacred place stirs the urge to leave a token—some echo of gratitude or prayer. Traditional offerings once blended into the land: milk poured at the roots of trees, wildflower petals returned to the grass, a little bread crumbled for birds. These gifts were part of life, shared among people, animals, and earth. Today, even a tiny object can upset fragile balance. The best offering may be invisible: a moment of silence, a song given gently to the wind, mindful care taken to remove a scrap of litter left behind. When you feel called to give something material, choose only what the land offers freely and in abundance—never rare flowers, branches, or stones that belong where they rest. Skip coins (metal poisons water and crowds the magic from wells), tea lights (risk fire, scatter wax and metal), synthetic ribbons (strangle birds and linger for decades), and anything that won't quickly return to soil. In the reciprocity spirit you first met when learning about land relationships in Chapter 3, real offerings leave places lighter and healthier, not burdened by our longing to connect.

Consult Local Guidance: Site Knowledge and Community Respect

Each sacred site carries its own story, rules, and needs. Look for posted guidance; signs reflect both conservation realities and ongoing cultural relationships. If there's no formal sign, it doesn't mean the place is up for grabs—locals often know unwritten etiquette, sensitive times, or areas needing rest. Whenever possible, talk to land stewards, community members, or visitor centers. A simple question like, "I'd like to visit [site] respectfully—are there customs or concerns I should know?" shows humility and readiness to learn. Sometimes access is limited because a site needs recovery or hosts ceremonies. In these cases, choosing to step back honors present-day guardianship, not just ancient tradition. This echoes principles found throughout modern heritage work, such as community-based approaches to sacred site management that center local voices and participation (Banda et al., 2024). You might discover alternative locations or ways to engage through local people—all building real relationship, not just consumption.

Documentation with Humility: Sharing Without Harm

Many of us want to capture the beauty of a holy well or record a storm's dance over standing stones. Still, sharing images or precise locations online often draws curious crowds who skip the context and caretaking. When you photograph, focus on close-up textures, shifting light, or personal experiences rather than wide shots that reveal locations. Ask permission before photographing people, ceremonies, or private spaces; credit those who share stories or guidance with you, and honor requests for privacy. Public heritage sites designed for education benefit from thoughtful sharing—visitor numbers support conservation work—but vulnerable places easily become overwhelmed. Remember to treat documentation as a tool for deepening your own sense of place, not just producing content for others. These steps build on the reciprocity ethics that run through this book and anticipate more detailed guidelines coming in Chapter 9, showing that authentic practice means guiding your actions by care and awareness.

Treating stones, waters, and skies as living partners means tending to their physical forms. Every act of care—from staying on paths to asking questions, leaving no trace to savoring the experience without broadcast—makes you an ancestor to future travelers and dreamers.

Bringing It All Together

Walking through landscapes marked by stones, wells, and shifting skies, it becomes clear that old ways of reading the world are still with us. Whether tracing the edge of a parish by boulder or noticing the warning in a cloud's shape, each gesture connects us to stories much older than any map or app. These practices have never just been about knowledge or survival—they're about relationship: to place, to memory, and to one another. The land speaks in many languages, from weather lore and folk ritual to the silent testimony of granite and water. Every offering, every story told at a stone or spring, keeps these threads alive, helping us find our bearings not only on the path but within ourselves.

As we move into the present, tending to these sacred places—by staying on paths, making mindful offerings, or simply pausing to listen—becomes an act of care, both for heritage and for our communities now. The technologies may change, but our longing for orientation, protection, and meaning remains constant. Stones, waters, and skies invite us to slow down and notice, to witness the layers of connection beneath our feet and above our heads. By practicing respect, curiosity, and humility, we help make sure these living relationships endure for future generations.

Chapter 7: Hearth and Threshold: Household Protections and Blessings

On a rain-soaked evening in a cozy stone cottage, the power flickers and dims, drawing the family naturally closer to the warm glow of the stove. Nearby, a heel of bread rests quietly on the mantel, placed there "for luck," while a worn horseshoe hangs crookedly above the door, and the baby's cradle bears a small red thread looped around its handle. These objects, passed down through generations, carry their meaning silently —less explained than simply accepted as part of the home's fabric. As the family settles in, their chatter drifts into stories: tales of how grandmother carefully banked embers each night to keep the fire alive, memories of new neighbors arriving with gifts of bread and salt, and recollections of the cattle fair that once came alongside a springtime bonfire's smoky embrace.

This familiar scene invites us to step into a moment where everyday acts around the hearth and threshold are more than routine — they are threads woven into centuries of care, protection, and blessings in Celtic life. From the humble blessings whispered over dwindling embers to the quiet placing of tokens at the doorway, these household customs reveal a deep connection between home, community, and the natural world. This chapter opens by tracing how the hearth became the sacred heart of domestic life, offering warmth and safety, and how the thresholds marked lines where welcome met watchfulness, all shaping a lived experience rich in meaning and mindful presence.

The Hearth as Sacred Center

During a storm, a family circles their stove, taking comfort in the old bread resting on the mantel and the red thread tied to a cradle. These objects anchor an ordinary evening, yet they also carry layers of meaning shaped by years of tradition. In many Scottish and Irish homes throughout the 19th century, such scenes meant more than shelter—they marked the hearth as the living heart of domestic life (Campbell, 1895/2012). The flickering fire, with its gentle warmth and steady rhythm, set the pulse for every meal, gathering, and story. Around this central flame, people practiced rituals that blended necessity with reverence, turning daily chores into connection points between family, ancestors, and the world beyond the walls.

Fire-keeping formed the daily foundation of this connection. Tending the coals at night, often by carefully banking them beneath a blanket of ash, kept the flame alive until morning. In Gaelic-speaking areas, the last person awake would whisper blessing words over the embers, treating their preservation as both duty and privilege (Carmichael, 1928). Losing the fire risked more than cold fingers; it might hint at neglect or worse, invite misfortune. A hearth grown cold could signal sickness, absence, or even death within, while a thriving fire suggested health and social standing. When moving to a new home, families sometimes carried live coals from their old hearth to kindle the first flames in the new one—a gesture acknowledging both continuity and hope (Gregor, 1881; Carmichael, 1900). Seasonal rekindling of the fire, especially during springtime festivals like Imbolc, connected personal routines to the larger rhythms outdoors. Lighting a fresh blaze could recall the solar cycles celebrated in earlier chapters, bringing the turning of the natural world right into the center of the dwelling.

Welcoming others became an act of both hospitality and protection at the hearthside. Offering bread, pouring milk, or simply making room by the stove showed more than good manners; it wove every visitor into the ongoing fabric of household blessing (McNeill, 1957). To share food or drink in the glow of the fire was to recognize common vulnerability, but also to declare goodwill. Blessings—whether whispered prayers or silent wishes—were believed to linger in the smoky air, protecting host and guest alike. In some homes, a piece of bread left on the mantel or a cup kept on hand for wayfarers stood as quiet tokens of readiness to welcome fortune or guard against harm (Evans-Wentz, 1911/1973). Just as offerings at wells acknowledged place-spirits, hospitality at the hearth recognized the sacredness of human connection and balanced individual needs with communal responsibility.

Night after night, stories echoed across the hearthspace. Children nestled close, elders spun tales, and neighbors pieced

Chapter 7: Hearth and Threshold: Household Protections and Blessings

together memory and wisdom by firelight. Story circles did more than pass the time—they kept alive a living oral tradition that shaped values and reminded listeners of seasonal change, local lore, and moral boundaries (Bruford, 1994). Patterns emerged: journeys begun and completed, bargains struck at thresholds, warnings about pride or generosity. The humble fireside became a classroom without books, teaching when to act, when to wait, and how to notice the thick weave of everyday relationships. The seasonal rekindling of fire mirrored the calendar cycles we explored earlier, bringing those rhythms into the home.

Meanings sparked even in the quiet ends of the evening, when someone read omens in the ash or puzzled over a stray coal found smoldering in the morning. In the Western Isles, people sometimes watched how sparks danced or noticed shapes left in soot, trading gentle predictions about luck or warning of change (Carmichael, 1900; McNeill, 1957). These readings were less about rigid rules and more about noticing patterns, letting the hearth's residue hint at joys or trials ahead. This sort of folk commentary gave everyone a role in interpreting the household's fortunes. The hearth's inward glow was balanced by vigilance at the edges, where thresholds required their own care and attention, drawing a line between safety and the unpredictable world outside.

Threshold Customs and Safeguards

Hearth fires glowed at the center of Celtic households, drawing family close in warmth and kinship. At the same time, that circle of care had limits—every home had edges where welcome and vulnerability met. Doorways, windows, and entryways marked these boundaries, shaping how people managed risk and connection to those beyond their walls.

Iron objects became familiar guardians at thresholds. Smiths held an honored place in Celtic culture: they transformed raw iron by fire and skill into sturdy tools or horseshoes, shaping the very symbols that households trusted for protection (Ellis, 1999). Placing a horseshoe above the door was more than decoration. The weight and chill of the metal spoke to the enduring power believed to keep harm at bay. Position mattered—points-up was widely said to "hold" luck inside, while points-down let it spill over those who entered. Nails hammered through lentils or frames did double duty; they secured wood but also anchored intent, joining practical carpentry with apotropaic purpose. These gestures turned craftsmanship itself into daily warding, blending what was useful with what felt necessary for safety (Green, 1995).

Rowan showed up wherever the air between inside and out grew thin. Known in Gaelic as caorann, this tree carried a reputation for guarding against ill will and witchcraft, especially at thresholds (Briggs, 1976). Its slender twigs and

Chapter 7: Hearth and Threshold: Household Protections and Blessings

bright red berries signaled vibrancy within ordinary reach. Households tucked bits of rowan above windows and doors, sometimes binding them with a thread dyed red. Red stood out—alert, lively, unmistakable—serving as visible tokens of watchfulness. Tying a thread into a knot offered a simple reminder to attend to comings and goings. None of these tokens announced themselves as sacred; a twist of yarn, a sprig on the sill, slipped right alongside workaday tools and sweeping brooms, easy to miss unless one looked closely. Chapter 5 touched on the plant's lore, yet here the meaning deepened at the very thresholds where belonging and danger pressed closest.

Sweeping routines shaped boundaries as much as locks or latches. Each morning, women swept dust from corners inward toward the hearth, gathering what belonged before sending debris outward, past the threshold. The order mattered. Clearing away old ashes last—a final sweep across the lintel—signaled both tidiness and the expulsion of unwelcome energies. These rhythms framed cleaning as more than labor; each movement aligned the household, reinforcing which side of the boundary was meant for keeping, which for letting go. Stories linger about such habits—one tells how a woman would gather crumbs and sweepings in her apron, then walk them out the front door with a silent wish that all trouble go with them (MacNeill, 1959). The threshold became a liminal space—a seam between domains—where gesture and intention worked together to define what stayed and what left.

First crossings into a new home carried layered meaning. When a family stepped over a fresh threshold, neighbors gathered with gifts: bread for sustenance, salt for wisdom and preservation. Bread broken and shared echoed hopes that no one would go hungry; salt reminded all present of lasting friendship and honor. The lighting of a first fire brought warmth not only to bodies, but also to relationships forged in witness (Danaher, 1972). Young and old alike took part, so the act stitched the home into the local fabric from the beginning. Even the simplest loaf and pinch of salt handed across the door made manifest a communal promise—that the household was not alone at its edge, but surrounded by eyes and hearts ready to stand guard.

Once these outer defenses found their shape—iron fixed, rowan hidden, floors swept, and new homes welcomed—the gaze of householders often shifted again. Attention turned inward, seeking ways to extend mindful protection to those most vulnerable: newborns in cradles, animals in byres, anyone whose safety needed gentle watching-over. These boundary practices laid the groundwork for caring for life's tender arrivals and dependents, signaling that every threshold safeguarded something precious.

Cradle and Cattle Protections

Having secured thresholds and boundaries, communities turned their protective attention to the most vulnerable beings within and around the home. Infants resting in cradles and livestock gathered in byres could mean the difference between a thriving family and hardship. Their survival carried both emotional bonds and practical consequences for everyone in the household. People saw care for children and animals not as private tasks but as shared responsibilities that linked families across generations, seasons, and neighborhoods. Stories about safeguarding these lives reveal how protection shaped community rhythms and fostered networks of accountability.

Naming and Blessing

The moment a child entered the world, neighbors and kin gathered to witness their arrival, joining in naming ceremonies shaped by local custom (Ó Catháin, 1995). In some Irish communities, baptismal water or water touched to church relics blessed infants before names were spoken aloud. This act marked more than an individual beginning—it made public the ties holding each family to its wider network. Invoking saints' names echoed hopes for guidance and gentle favor, but the heart of the practice lay in the gathering itself. Neighbors pledged watchfulness, brought gifts, and shared stories about lineage and obligation. These occasions confirmed responsibilities well beyond immediate parents; older siblings, godparents, friends, and even distant relatives heard tales reminding them all to step in when needed. The ceremony's ritual gestures created circles of care and strengthened memory, quietly distributing the work of vigilance and kindness across many hands (Ó Catháin, 1995).

Beltane Smoke

As spring warmed the land, Scottish and Irish farming communities prepared for the shift to open pastures. With grass lush and days stretching longer, collective attention moved to the cattle whose health meant prosperity for all (Danaher, 1972). At Beltane, villagers built carefully tended fires, sometimes set in parallel so herds could pass between the smoke. Swirling air and the scent of peat or turf carried hopes for safety through the grazing season. Many hands fed the flames and guided animals, turning the act into coordinated labor. Beltane fire customs timed with practical needs: only after the threat of late frost would cows leave the shelter of winter byres. Accounts describe villagers dousing torches at the finish, then sharing food and watching for omens—ritual and routine mingled as a way to make risk manageable together. Rather than personal magic, these smoky processions reflected seasonal teamwork and shared investment in survival (Danaher, 1972).

Amulets and Pins

On ordinary days, mothers and herders tucked pins, buttons, or bits of colored yarn near sleeping babies or prized animals' stalls. These objects gained meaning through attention: the act of pinning, placing, or knotting signaled alertness and intention, more than any material value (Wood-Martin, 1901). Visible near a cradle, a pin acted as a silent prompt to double-check blankets or check on a child's breathing. A bright button tied above a calf's head reminded caretakers to pause during chores. While regional folklore sometimes told of special stones or iron charms, everyday protections relied mostly on familiar, humble items at hand. Community knowledge stressed that tokens did not replace skill or diligence—rather, they anchored focus amid busy routines. For both infants and livestock, these practices kept vulnerability at the center of household attention without creating a sense of magical certainty (Wood-Martin, 1901).

Night Vigil Tales

When danger felt nearest—in the hush after midnight births or the uncertain hours of animal illness—neighbors often took turns keeping watch. Stories from rural Ireland and the Scottish Highlands speak of company steadying the mood during long nights (Evans, 1957). A lamp burned low while two or three sat near the cradle, sharing quiet talk or song to keep everyone alert. In the byre, someone sang softly as calves arrived, ready to fetch help or comfort anxious parents. These vigils were as much social gatherings as they were acts of protection; companionship guarded against fear and fatigue. Storytelling often filled these hours, passing time and offering reassurance through repetition of well-known legends or recent happenings. Through such shared effort, individuals became part of a living network, protecting not just the family inside but the whole web of households nearby (Evans, 1957).

These customs invite us to notice where care concentrates in our own homes and communities. Stories of cradle and cattle protections reveal ongoing patterns of attention, shared labor, and seasonal mindfulness—threads readers will trace through the reflective exercises to come.

Interpreting Household Signs

Stepping from the histories of cradle and cattle protections into the world you move through each day, you're invited to explore your own home as a living, breathing place of gathering and boundary. Earlier sections have shown how watchfulness and everyday care formed the backbone of household blessing; that same attentiveness can shape daily life now, with observation taking the lead instead of imitation. By focusing on the present—on where light falls, how food appears or disappears, and who crosses thresholds—you nurture an awareness that roots you in place, honoring both history and your own context.

Light and Draft Mapping

Take one week to gently notice the way sunlight filters and air moves through your main living space. You only need a sheet of paper for a simple floor sketch, a notebook, and an openness to what unfolds. Let routines carry on as usual—no need to rearrange anything. On your sketch, mark three times each day: morning, midday, and evening. Where does natural light linger? Which corners draw brightness, and which fall into shadow? As you walk the rooms, pause where you sense drafts—a quick chill by a window, the whisper near a door, or a steady current from a vent. Draw these pathways onto your floor sketch. Sound shapes a space, too: listen during quiet hours, busy bursts, and those liminal late nights. Where do footsteps echo? Which walls catch street noise or laughter? Note these sound paths alongside light and draft markings. At week's end, reflect: How did these patterns shape where people gather or slip away? Where does comfort draw you in, or movement nudge you along? Light and breeze might form their own natural thresholds, channeling warmth or inviting pause just as much as any built hearth or threshold once did (Ó Súilleabháin, 1977). Your observations matter; there are no right answers—only your growing skill at seeing what is already present.

Seasonal Food Notes

Your kitchen forms another kind of map, holding stories that follow the seasons without you needing special knowledge. Over three months, keep a short log at the start of each month. Jot down five to seven foods you find yourself buying or reaching for most: maybe it's hearty soups and root vegetables while winter lingers, then lighter salads or the first strawberries as spring arrives. Notice which staples stay—rice or beans, oil or spices—and which rotate with the time of year. If you're sharing space, let everyone add a favorite. Choose a couple foods from your list and write a line about a memory or tradition they bring: perhaps soup recalls a friend's visit, or canned peaches tie back to a family market. When three months pass, look over your notes. How do these rhythms mirror the wider world outside your window? Which items feel so tied to home that you would pack them if you had to move, offering a quiet echo of bread-and-salt customs used to welcome new beginnings (Evans-Wentz, 1911)? Notice patterns in meals not as old rites to be copied, but as windows into continuity, care, and community, all shaped by your own needs and resources.

Doorway Journal

The doorway carries weight—a place of welcome, parting, excitement, or calm. For three days, keep a small notebook near your main entrance. Whenever someone enters or leaves—whether that's flatmates, family, deliveries, pets, or even a shift in weather—jot down what you notice. Who or what crossed over? Did chatter bloom, did energy stall, or did the room hush? Write a sentence about the feeling in that moment—anticipation, relief, irritation, gladness. Record departures, too: does quiet return, or something linger unresolved? After three days, reread your notes. What regularities stand out around welcome and boundaries? How do you naturally mark the shift between inside and out, between work and rest or solitude and company? These points of entry already shape the flow of household life, echoing the threshold customs of earlier eras without requiring ritual—the attention itself is its own form of stewardship (Danaher, 1995). Home, in this way, stays alive to change and connection.

Ethical Boundaries and Reflective Practice

As you move through these exercises, hold ethical awareness at every step. The goal here isn't to replicate Irish, Scottish, Welsh, or Breton household customs, but to practice presence, discernment, and care within your own context. Let your observations belong to you. If you share insights or patterns with others, cite your inspiration and steer friends toward folklore archives and cultural museums rather than stories stripped of their meaning (Danaher, 2011). Learning through noticing builds humility, respect, and readiness to meet neighbors, visitors, and the land itself with hospitality and responsibility. These tools prepare you to journey further without pretending to carry traditions that aren't yours. Start slow, listen well, and trust that insight grows from paying attention—not from performance. This approach aligns closely with the values of local relationship and relational magic that have run quietly through every chapter (Ó Súilleabháin, 1977).

Bringing It All Together

Stepping back, it's clear how small gestures—banking a fire, setting bread on the mantel, or tying red thread to a cradle—have long shaped the fabric of home life across Celtic cultures. These habits weren't just old routines; they were ways families cared for one another, welcomed guests, and kept a watchful eye on both what was precious and what might bring risk. The hearth wasn't only a place for warmth or cooking, but a quiet center of blessing where stories, laughter, and worries blended together in the flicker of firelight. At the same time, boundaries like doors and windows became spaces of both hospitality and protection, marked by simple tokens like horseshoes or rowan twigs. Through caring acts and practical magic at thresholds, homes held together family, memory, and community.

So many patterns you've read about—sweeping floors, sharing food with neighbors, or keeping a gentle vigil over babies and cattle—revealed deeper values of responsibility and connection. These customs all pointed to the idea that household care isn't just about physical safety, but also about creating spaces of trust and belonging. Even now, using observation and intention lets anyone shape their living space into something meaningful, without copying traditions that aren't theirs. By paying attention to light, movement, food, and the flow of people, you add your own threads to the cloth of home. In honoring what's present and being mindful about your choices, you take part in the same circle of care that has welcomed, protected, and guided people through stormy nights and ordinary days alike.

Chapter 8: Tokens, Threads, and Tools: Objects with Story

Have you ever held a bronze pendant patterned with intricate Celtic knots, wondering if it carried some hidden power? Perhaps you bought it from an online shop or picked it up at a craft fair, drawn to its design alone. Yet, when that same knotwork is stamped out by the thousands in a factory, does it still feel meaningful? Compare it to a small pin dipped in holy water from a local well, or a cross woven carefully from rushes on the eve of a saint's feast and hung in a farmhouse doorway. These objects carry stories—their strength built not from metal or shape but from layers of blessing, family care, and connection to place. It's in what people say over them, how they're used and treasured, that their true meaning grows.

This idea that objects gather significance through lived experience opens a window into Celtic folk traditions. Here, charms and amulets are more than simple trinkets; they are vessels shaped by story, community, and time. As we step into this chapter, we'll look closely at how everyday items become charged with meaning, how rituals and blessings intertwine with making and carrying these tokens, and why the context around an object matters just as much as the object itself. By understanding this, we can appreciate why a factory-made pendant will never quite hold the same weight as one made with intention and rooted deeply in tradition.

Chapter 8: Tokens, Threads, and Tools: Objects with Story

Charms and Amulets in Context

Picture that shiny bronze pendant stamped with Celtic knots—maybe you've seen it on a market stall or worn one yourself. It feels heavy in your hand, but the power you seek isn't built into the design or metal. Remember the protective tokens from the last chapter: the safety pin tucked inside a curtain hem or the rush cross set over a front door. These objects gained their strength not from what they were made of, but from the stories carried alongside them, the prayers whispered as they hung, and the ordinary hands that put them in place.

Story-Imbued Meaning

In a warm kitchen, a grandmother stands by the hearth every evening and lifts an old brass pin between her fingers. She tells the story again—how her own mother placed this very pin at each grandchild's cradle, how it guarded restless babies, how the family believes no harm ever came to anyone under its gaze. Neighbors nod knowingly, children are hushed, and the tale becomes part of household memory. The pin itself grows weightier with each retelling, moving beyond simple metal to become an anchor for belonging and hope. When visitors see the pin, it's more than decoration; it's a thread tying loved ones and generations. This is how birth charms and family amulets root into local identity (Ó hÓgáin, 1999). Anonymous pins bought in bulk don't spark stories or draw community care—power arises through shared experience.

Blessing Pathways

Stories live alongside acts of blessing. Some tokens take on meaning when dipped in water from a local holy well, wrapped and tied to tree branches as prayers for healing. People bring tokens and cloths, each chosen with intention, and let the cold stream run over their hands before giving thanks. At seasonal fires—Beltane in spring or Samhain in autumn—families might pass ribbons or cords through fragrant smoke, murmuring words of protection learned from elders. You saw these patterns back in Chapter 4. Blessings spoken aloud tend to be short and loving, not commanding but aligning object and owner with care. Someone might simply say, "May you watch over her," while knotting a red string at the cradle. Each act accumulates meaning: water, fire, or word, all grounded in presence rather than spectacle. Patterns emerge here too, as we'll see when we examine weaving traditions and shapes that carry intention within homes (Ó Catháin & Smyth, 2003).

Everyday Materials

Material hardly matters—rushes, pins, cords, shells—all become vessels for care because of their journey. When families gather at Imbolc to weave a simple cross from soft green rushes, timing is everything. Rushes cut that morning, voices raised together, and a threshold waiting for the new cross: this is what gives the object meaning. A cord knotted before a long trip, a shell picked up on a windy shore and carried home as a promise—these humble things hold vows and memories only because of the moments spent with them. Ordinary items turn special with blessing and story, never because they're rare or exotic (Ó hÓgáin, 2002). Their magic comes from relationship: to place, to moment, to person who gives and receives.

Caution on Commerce

As you continue your journey, it's easy to feel drawn to mass-produced "Celtic" jewelry or ornaments, and there's no shame in wanting beautiful things that speak to your roots or interests. Yet much is lost in factory replication: the artisan's hand fades, the story behind each item vanishes, and ethical questions about source and purpose arise. Local work—like a handmade St. Brigid's cross woven in a neighbor's kitchen—retains living connection, while anonymous pendants struggle to carry more than surface pattern. Ask who benefits when you buy: does your purchase feed back into community, honor the tradition, and support craftspeople you can name? Seek sellers who credit their sources, use local materials, or invite you into the process. Making something yourself, receiving a piece from family, or supporting small makers creates pathways for meaning far stronger than anything offered by the marketplace alone (MacNeill, 1962). Blessings, as we'll explore later in this chapter, do not stick to metal or fabric unless intent and relationship guide every step of the making. As form and pattern come into focus, notice how knots, braids, and twists add yet another voice to the story—the next section will show how the way an object is shaped further deepens its presence.

Knots, Patterns, and Weaving

Objects in folk practice hold their meaning through the stories and relationships that shape them, not by any energy locked inside. When hands twist a cord or plait rushes together, every pattern remembers an agreement—a promise spoken aloud, a hope shared quietly, or a blessing murmured while working. This move from seeing objects as holding power on their own to recognizing the relationships woven into their making changes how crafted things are honored. In Celtic traditions, the very act of tying, braiding, and weaving is a language, telling stories not just about what was made, but why and with whom.

Binding and Loosing: Ethics and Practice

Knot-work in these traditions never aimed at control for its own sake. Instead, binding and loosing were symbolic acts carried out with consent, trust, and care. A cord tied around the wrist marked a bond between friends, lovers, or parent and child—not a spell worked over someone, but a visible sign of connection forged together. During festivals or family ceremonies, threads might be knotted one by one, each knot carrying a spoken wish or shared value. If a fear or illness troubled the household, untying knots became part of gentle release. A neighbor or community healer might sit beside someone, slowly undoing a cord while offering quiet words, showing respect for boundaries and permission at every step.

Historical sources remind us that these practices required clear agreements (Ó Giolláin, 2000). Any attempt to use knot magic without mutual understanding would have gone against social norms and the ethical codes of Gaelic and Brythonic communities. In some Scottish Highland households, mothers tied protective strings for children with words of blessing, then later helped untie them when danger had passed—always in the open, always within relationship (Mac Coitir, 2017). Protective house charms described in Chapter 7 often involved braided straw or reed crosses placed above doors, where their presence depended on both human intent and seasonal timing.

Protective Weaves and Insular Art Echoes

Everyday objects also took on power through woven crossings. Reed baskets sat beside cottage doors, catching early light and breaking up shadows thought to carry harm. Straw mats stretched across thresholds formed crisscrossed patterns meant to confuse ill-wishing spirits and mark a safe passage into the home. In Welsh farms, springtime braids hung near hearths or barn beams to draw in blessing during lambing, their freshness a yearly renewal echoing the seasons (Evans-Wentz, 1911).

The timing often mattered as much as the pattern. For instance, Brigid's crosses—plaited each Imbolc in Ireland—carried the hopes of a new season, honoring saints and ancestors while refreshing the commitment to protect home and kin. Similar customs appeared at Lughnasa and other harvest times, when new weavings would replace the old.

Alongside these household crafts, spiral and interlace motifs echoed across carved sticks, embroidered borders, or edges of door lintels. Spirals marked the turning of time or personal journeys, while interlace—with no clear beginning or end—mirrored beliefs about the web of life and return. But each region spoke this visual language a bit differently. The Irish triskele could be linked to movement and progress, while Scottish versions circulated in tales of water spirits or ancestral memory. On Manx walking staffs, distinctive three-armed spirals called triskellion appeared, tied to local legends about sea crossings. Welsh carving often favored chevrons and zigzag lines, which guarded entries and marked ritual sites. While these designs may look similar edge to edge, only careful learning reveals names, meanings, and stories rooted in place (Foster & Lichfield, 1998). It's best to approach with curiosity rather than assumption, since what looks like "Celtic" knotwork may hold several worlds of difference along the strands.

Craft Transmission: Living Knowledge

No book can pass on the whole art of weaving cords or reading threshold patterns. Traditions lived through handing down technique—grandmother to grandchild, neighbors sharing skill over tea, friends gathering at festival time. Each person's way of twisting, braiding, or knotting spoke of their lineage and of small variations treasured within families. Learning meant not only repeating movements but knowing when green rushes softened after rain, or when the waxing moon called out for blessings to be made.

Story moved alongside skill—the right time to thank the willow or gather grass, the blessing spoken before starting, or the song sung as hands plied the thread. This web of knowledge shaped both object and maker. Though factory-made cords or baskets can mimic forms, they cannot carry the gratitude, stories, and connections built up over years (Hunter, 1976). Woven craft holds more than utility; it holds memory, intention, and the feel of loved hands moving together through familiar patterns. Just as fingers guide fiber into form, so voices shape meaning into sound—a reminder as we turn next to blessings carried on words and rhythm.

References

Evans-Wentz, W.Y. (1911). The Fairy Faith in Celtic Countries. Oxford University Press.
Foster, S., & Lichfield, G. (1998). The Book of Celtic Magic.

Llewellyn Publications.

Hunter, J. (1976). The Fiddle and the Frame: Folk Traditions of Scotland. John Donald Publishers.

Mac Coitir, N. (2017). Irish Nature: Myths, Legends, and Folklore. The Collins Press.

Ó Giolláin, D. (2000). Locating Irish Folklore: Tradition, Modernity, Identity. Cork University Press.

Music, Word, and Blessing

Just as knots and weaves carry meaning through their making, words spoken or sung wrap memory and care around a moment. Picture a parent in an old stone cottage, holding a child flushed with fever. The parent whispers a short rhyme, its lines simple and repeating: a pattern passed down from grandmother to mother. The rhythm of these words settles the breath, both for the speaker and the little one listening. Repeated patterns act like memory hooks—when fear makes it hard to think, a four-line charm with easy-to-match endings is what stays. Fisherfolk, too, would recite blessings before heading out to sea, letting familiar phrases steady anxious hearts as boats slipped from shore. Meter—the deliberate beat of the words—does more than sound pleasing: it brings order. When life feels uncertain, pattern and predictability help give comfort. Rhyme provides handles for the mind to grip, so even when stress tries to scatter thought, the shape of the language holds together.

Call-and-response forms bring this structure into community. Imagine the pounding of wool during a waulking session. As women work the cloth, a lead singer chants and others reply, voices rising and falling in a tide. Each response shares the emotional burden, moving attention from solitary worry to shared purpose. This isn't just poetic tradition—it's practical. Song keeps hands working in time and reminds each person they aren't alone. Participation shapes belonging, reinforcing social ties and, over time, helping whole communities remember and repeat vital knowledge (Newton, 1996).

The blending of languages within these charms and songs tells its own story. In many Celtic regions, charms hand down generations blend old tongue and newer words. Irish "sláinte" (meaning health) or Scottish Gaelic "beannachd" (blessing) often appear mid-sentence in English prayers. Sometimes a verse will begin by invoking saints in English but slip into the original dialect for place-names or final wishes. This bilingual texture isn't accidental; it grew from centuries of encounter between local ways and imported religion or administration (Ó Giolláin, 2000). For diaspora communities, even a single word in the ancestral language can create a powerful bridge. Saying "sláinte" at a family table links you to people and places that shaped its sound. Careful notation of dialect and pronunciation matters here, not only for accuracy but as an act of respect. These choices honor those who first spoke or sang the words and prevent the flattening of nuance.

Occupational songs braided blessing directly into daily labor. Think of rowing crews chanting as oars dip in unison, or millers' voices matching the turn of grindstones. In the Hebrides and Highlands, waulking songs kept time for wet cloth beaten smooth, each verse wishing for health, fair weather, or safe homecoming. These were never separate ceremonies tucked away for special days—they came alive in the sweat and laughter of shared work. Singing together made the labor lighter and built mutual care. One voice began, others joined, until everyone felt seen and supported. This weaving of blessing and necessity isn't unique to the Celtic world—barn-raising songs on American farms or sea shanties share the same spirit. What matters is how rhythm and group participation transform hard tasks into moments of connection (Siren, 2017).

When it comes to sharing these verbal traditions today, care and ethics matter as much as memory. Attribution is more than a formality—it's a way of keeping the thread unbroken. When quoting a historical charm or song, pause to ask: Who collected it? Who said it first, and where? If you find a charm in a printed collection, note the speaker and date if possible—this lets others follow your path back through time. There's also a difference in permission. A phrase whispered in a kitchen carries different weight than a festival chant echoed in public. If you're learning from a living tradition—still spoken in modern homes or gatherings—seek consent before sharing outside, or use paraphrase with clear credit. This approach honors both the people and histories behind the words (Shaw, 2012). Ask yourself before passing any charm onward: Who recorded this? Was it meant for everyone's ears, or just family? Is the tradition still in practice? Have I reached out to those who steward it today? Transparent sharing invites continued relationship rather than silent extraction.

Understanding how these verbal traditions functioned historically prepares us to meet them thoughtfully in our own lives. These principles of respectful transmission become especially important when we consider how to engage with traditional objects and words today. As you look ahead, remember that every spoken or sung blessing holds both the care of its givers and the responsibility of its keepers.

Objects in Modern Contexts

Building on the careful attribution practices we explored with verbal charms, we need to bring the same mindful respect to physical objects. Just as words gather meaning through story and relationship, so do crafted items—meaning comes from context, not copying. When you work with objects rooted in living Celtic traditions, your choices matter: who makes them, with what materlals, why, and how those stories travel forward.

Local Craft Support

Commissioning work from regional artisans builds living traditions. When you order a woven cloth or a carved token from someone within the culture, you do more than buy an item—you invest in the survival of skills that might otherwise fade. Supporting craftspeople pays for their time and encourages younger generations to learn the trade. These makers act as culture bearers, holding knowledge that links language, land, and history. A simple exchange becomes community support when you ask about the meaning behind motifs, seek advice about respectful use, or learn how an object fits into seasonal practice. A good commissioning conversation involves sharing your intentions openly, asking about regional differences, and listening closely if a maker says a design is meant only for certain occasions. Always pay fairly and credit the artisan by name, region, and craft tradition when sharing images or stories with others (VAI_Projects, 2025). This visibility helps future customers find authentic sources and tells artisans their work matters beyond the local market.

Material Sourcing

The relational approach to land we explored in Chapter 3 extends to how we source materials. Objects gain meaning when they connect to their home ground. Choosing locally grown plant fibers or wool from named flocks ties your work into the textures and stories of place. For Irish folk practice, linen spun from flax grown nearby holds stories different from imported cotton; Scottish traditions carry the scent and memory of local sheep breeds. Even when traditional material isn't available, look for equivalents shaped by the same climate—a reed basket made from abundant willow feels more at home than one from rare imported cane. Don't use endangered heritage materials just because they seem authentic. Harvesting scarce items undermines the continuity you hope to honor. Instead, document where each element came from, as carefully as you can (VAI_Projects, 2025). When you record the farm, county, or woods linked to your materials, you create a living chain between your work and the landscapes that make it possible. In some cases, adaptation shows care: finding a renewable source signals your commitment to sustainability and to the ongoing health of both tradition and ecosystem.

Non-Sacred Replicas

Replicas play a useful role for learning and teaching, but serve a different purpose than spiritual tools used in practice. Museum pieces and classroom replicas allow sacred originals to stay safe within communities. Label demonstration items clearly. Add a card or note: "Interpretive replica, inspired by [region/tradition]." Include a short explanation of the original's role, like "The Brigid's Cross shown here demonstrates weaving, but does not hold blessing power." Ask culture bearers—people active in the community—what details are right to share. Some decorative patterns or techniques may be public, while sacred markings or ritual methods should remain private. You might create a clootie offering for display out of biodegradable scraps, with signage explaining the real practice and its proper contexts. Clarity and consultation help protect meaning while opening doors for respectful education (VAI_Projects, 2025).

Documentation Practices

Honoring the story of an object takes more than labeling or cataloguing—it means caring about what will be remembered. Keep a small card or file for each piece, noting who made it, when, where, what materials were used, and why it was created. Photograph it in its home setting: a mantle, window ledge, or field at harvest. Record which song accompanied its making, or any blessings spoken over it. Layered notes—such as the season a rush cross was woven, or the village where wool was dyed—add richness for anyone who inherits or studies these pieces later. When possible, pass this documentation along with the object itself. Future caretakers, family, or museums will understand its story and handle it with insight. This practice also prepares you for deeper ethical frameworks in Chapter 9, building habits of transparency and stewardship that keep meaning alive even as objects travel (VAI_Projects, 2025).

Returning again and again to story, relationship, and context grounds all these choices. Slowing down, listening, learning from culture bearers, and accepting boundaries honors both the living traditions and the people who keep them. It's not only about what we can hold in our hands, but what we can sustain for the next person who reaches for meaning.

Bringing It All Together

As we've seen, the heart of these practices isn't found in shop-bought pendants or intricate patterns copied from books, but in the stories and relationships that grow around everyday objects. A simple pin passed through generations, a cross woven as a promise for the coming year, or a handful of words sung together at bedtime—these moments shape meaning far beyond what any factory can replicate. Whether it's a rush picked near home or a blessing whispered over a cord, it is care, context, and intention that turn an object into something powerful. Meaning forms through connection—with people, with place, and with the act itself.

When we think about bringing Celtic folk traditions into our own lives, it helps to remember that authenticity isn't measured by age or appearance, but by the web of relationships that support each item or ritual. Choosing to learn from culture bearers, support local makers, or simply weave your own story with respect and gratitude does more than honor the past—it keeps these living practices alive and meaningful. Trust the ordinary things—a ribbon, a rhyme, or a well-placed charm—to carry the weight of care you offer. What matters most is how we tend to these small acts of making and remembering, weaving them into the fabric of daily life.

Chapter 9: Boundaries and Belonging: Ethics for the Curious

When you ask online about a "Celtic protection charm," you might get a flood of different answers—some pointing to Irish blessings, others to Scottish knots or Breton designs. This mix-up isn't just confusing; it shows why we can't treat Celtic traditions as one single thing. Each region—whether Irish, Scottish, Welsh, or Breton—has its own stories, words, and ways of doing things. Recognizing these differences helps us see practices as connected to real places and people instead of blending everything into a vague idea. It's like learning that saying "Celtic" without more detail is a bit like calling all fruit simply "sweet stuff" and missing what makes each piece unique.

So how do we stay curious and respectful without crossing boundaries? This chapter digs into that question, starting with why no one practice can represent all Celtic traditions. We'll explore how honoring local names, languages, and the living communities behind these customs shapes ethical engagement. From understanding who holds the knowledge, to asking for permission, to sharing credit honestly—we look at ways to approach Celtic culture with care and thoughtfulness while keeping our genuine curiosity alive.

Avoiding Homogenization

As we saw in the opening example, asking for a "Celtic protection charm" online often results in a whirlwind of answers—one post points to an Irish blessing, another mentions Breton patterns, and someone else insists a Scottish knot is best. That confusion isn't just frustrating; it reveals why honoring regional boundaries matters. To avoid flattening centuries of living tradition into a single, mushy idea of "Celtic," you should start every description with the region—Irish, Scottish, Welsh, or Breton—and, if possible, the narrower place. Regional identifiers are not just boxes to check; they connect practices to landscape, language, and real people. For instance, saying "Irish household blessing from County Clare" instantly grounds a practice in the Atlantic coast's weather, Irish Gaelic language, and parish customs, helping you learn about where it comes from and who shaped it. Using loose labels like "Celtic charm" risks mixing bits from very different places, which can create invented blends with no known history (*The CR FAQ - an Introduction to Celtic Reconstructionist Paganism - Intermediate Questions*, 2025). Regional naming also lights a path toward reliable sources—local museums, folk archives, or actual communities—rather than mass-market "Celtic" shops.

Language is more than decoration. Names, terms, and pronunciations hold layers of meaning that translations rarely capture. Take the difference between Irish "holy wells" and Scottish "saints' wells." Both are springs honored by locals, but the Irish tradition often centers offerings to Brigid or unnamed spirits, while Scottish sites might link to saints adopted after Christianization. Even if the English words sound similar, their stories, devotional focus, and roles in the community can diverge. Learning the right way to say words shows respect, too. For example, "Samhain" is pronounced "SOW-win," not "sam-HANE." Accurate pronunciation signals care for language and the listeners whose heritage you hope to honor. Watch out for false friends: a "craig" in Scotland means a rock or crag, while "creig" in Wales might point to something quite different. When you write about a practice, include the original term with a short explanation—like "tobar" (Irish: well) or "ffynnon" (Welsh: spring)—so readers keep the feel of the language without losing clarity. This honors the people who still use these words in daily life and keeps relationships with living languages strong, without making anyone feel shut out (*The CR FAQ - an Introduction to Celtic Reconstructionist Paganism - Intermediate Questions*, 2025).

Remember how Chapter 5 described hawthorn customs shifting from Brittany's lowlands to Highland fields? Or how the seasonal rituals in Chapter 4 mirrored local climates and farming cycles? Those differences showed up for a reason. It's tempting to spot visual echoes—a protective knot here, a fire festival there—and imagine a unified Celtic system behind them all. Yet shared imagery doesn't mean identical meaning. For example, a knotted string pattern in rural Ireland may

Chapter 9: Boundaries and Belonging: Ethics for the Curious

protect cattle and the home's fortune, crafted each spring for Beltane. Over in a Scottish fishing village, a lookalike knot could be made from rope, blessed specifically to shelter boats and crews braving the North Sea. The shapes recall each other, but the materials, timing, and purpose are tied to the needs of each community. Stone veneration gives another case: in some areas, marked stones became healing shrines linked to saints and visited on pilgrimage days; elsewhere, nearly identical stones stand as boundary markers, woven into stories of clan land rather than physical health. When drawing parallels, always state both the resemblance and where things split. Notes like, "Similar in shape to Welsh healing stones, but here used to mark farm boundaries rather than for blessings," help everyone celebrate shared roots while recognizing lived diversity (*The CR FAQ - an Introduction to Celtic Reconstructionist Paganism - Intermediate Questions*, 2025).

Community knowledge holders set the standard for what is authentic, not outsiders looking in. Instead of relying on generic "Celtic spirituality" books, you'll get far more from fieldwork collections, regional folklore journals, or insights from someone named and placed "Róisín Ní Chonaill, County Kerry storyteller," for instance. Living memory matters: asking local elders, attending language group events, or visiting community museums keeps traditions rooted in present-day context. Archival records, like older ethnographic notes or folklore indexes, offer windows into past practice but may lack today's relevance, so always specify whether your information comes from living voices or historical documents. Good citation means naming the person, place, or institution involved, with permission wherever needed. Cultural organizations and language groups take great care to safeguard these traditions; referencing them acknowledges the networks that keep folk magic alive. Try not to impose outside frameworks—like neopagan systems or New Age theories—onto community practices that already have their own logic, authority, and rhythm. Tracing knowledge back to its human source is both scholarly and ethical, ensuring respect for those who carry these traditions forward (*The CR FAQ - an Introduction to Celtic Reconstructionist Paganism - Intermediate Questions*, 2025).

Once we understand why regional naming matters, we can examine who has access to these traditions and how power shapes that access—a question at the heart of the section ahead.

Power, Access, and Privilege

Respecting regional boundaries means recognizing that not all knowledge is equally accessible—and that access itself is shaped by history, privilege, and community protection. Building on regional awareness, permission protocols form the first line of ethical engagement in Celtic folk traditions. Imagine standing before a holy well you've read about or hearing an elder share a family charm at a local gathering. Before snapping a photo, recording a story, or reposting someone's craft online, pause to ask explicit permission from

Chapter 9: Boundaries and Belonging: Ethics for the Curious

everyone with a stake: the person sharing, any site custodian, and often, the broader community. Consent isn't just a checkbox; it's living respect for relationships that stretch across generations. If you're not sure whether your intentions are welcome or your documentation could go further than intended, always ask. Clarify: Will your photo be part of a private record or shared with others? Can an audio clip be used for teaching, or should it remain in your own notes? Document permissions—sometimes written, sometimes spoken—so those boundaries stay clear. These small moments build trust and protect everyone involved. It might feel awkward to make these requests, but reframing consent as a gesture of care moves past discomfort and toward shared safety. When someone asks for privacy, anonymizing details or omitting names lets stories travel while honoring the wishes of those who entrusted them to you (*Llygedyn Grove*, 2025).

Gatekeeping brings up difficult feelings for people drawn to learn more than they are offered. Being told that a story, a site, or a ritual is "not for you" can sting, raising questions about inclusion, fairness, and even heartbreak. Yet these closed doors usually signal care, not exclusion for its own sake. When knowledge rests behind community boundaries—like a family healing charm never written down, or a pilgrimage route kept quiet among locals—it's rarely about keeping people out. Instead, it's about shielding ancestral wisdom against harm: ecological damage where too many visitors trample sacred paths, spiritual dilution from copying rituals without understanding, or loss of meaning through careless retelling. Communities often balance protection with sharing by offering public festivals, interpretive centers, and published folklore collections instead of opening every circle. Hearing "this isn't for you" is less a personal rejection and more an invitation to find ways to engage that respect what cannot be given. Receiving what is freely shared and approaching limits with gratitude helps shift focus from ownership to stewardship (*Llygedyn Grove*, 2025).

Cultural sensitivities run deep in the landscapes and communities that hold Celtic folk practices. As we explored in earlier chapters on holy wells, standing stones, and household customs, these traditions didn't survive in safe isolation. Stories of language suppression, religious persecution, and forced assimilation have left lasting trauma throughout Celtic-speaking regions. Healers who keep charms within their families aren't hiding magic for power's sake—they're protecting inheritances that were once under threat. When you visit a graveyard or trace ancient routes with your own feet, step quietly. Let reverence shape your actions: avoid performative rituals for social media, and listen for local voices rather than centering your own experience. Sometimes, you won't get an explanation for these rules. Honor them anyway. Acknowledging pain and vulnerability isn't about seeking drama, but about carrying yourself with a respect that recognizes how much was nearly lost. Allow space for sites and stories to belong to local people longer than they belong to visitors. This approach may mean observing, listening, and supporting from the margins rather than insisting on participation (*Llygedyn Grove*, 2025).

Benefit sharing closes the ethical circle, moving beyond consumption to active reciprocity. When you learn from living Celtic tradition—whether through research, pilgrimages, or crafting—find tangible ways to give back. For those with means, donating to the maintenance funds of holy wells or caretakers of sacred landscapes supports the spaces that teach you. Buying books and crafts directly from regional creators amplifies local voices and economies. Even on a limited budget, you can contribute by supporting language revitalization programs or volunteering time for community projects. If you gain insight or material for your own teaching or writing, consider returning value through financial support or service. Sharing what you've learned also means amplifying the perspectives of tradition-bearers themselves, not just your interpretations. This kind of benefit sharing isn't payment for access—it's about returning value and building lasting connection. With these external protocols in place, the question becomes how to engage sincerely with what you've been given access to—without claiming authority you haven't earned (*Llygedyn Grove*, 2025).

Authenticity without Authority Claims

With an understanding of access and consent in place, we can now turn to how you present yourself and your learning in Celtic folk traditions. Authentic engagement requires not only sensitivity to history and permission but also clear honesty about your role as a learner rather than an authority. It's common to feel pressure to show mastery, especially in spaces where expertise is often measured by credentials or lineage claims. Yet, the heart of respectful participation lies in transparency, modesty, and honoring those who keep these traditions alive (Blackstock, 2024).

Transparency Statement: Name Your Learning Path and Limits

Naming how and where you've learned something builds trust and sets the right tone for ethical engagement. Instead of presenting information as ancient fact or personal revelation, anchor it clearly with real sources. For example, say "I learned this Brigid blessing from a recording collected in County Kildare in the 1970s," or "This household custom comes from my grandmother's stories in Glasgow." These statements build bridges between you and tradition rather than pretending at ownership or invention.

Being honest about gaps in your knowledge invites connection instead of competition. You might explain, "My family memory doesn't include this ritual, so I'm learning from archival books and local guides." This lets others know you're open to learning together, not claiming command over practices. If your relationship to a region is recent—say, you're a visitor or descendant living far away—naming that context grounds your perspective and prevents romanticizing or assuming closeness that isn't there. Gaps in knowledge are realistic and respected; everyone starts somewhere, and admitting limits shows care rather than weakness (Blackstock, 2024).

Contextual Practice: Keep Gestures Small and Respectful

Simple, local observance goes further than elaborate reenactment when it comes to genuine practice. Taking a walk outside on the equinox, tending a home altar with plants native to your area, or quietly observing seasonal changes all show care without spectacle. These small acts matter more than importing complex rituals out of context—such as recreating Irish well blessings in places with different ecosystems or histories. Such gestures can feel like imitation or strip away the meaning held by the land and its people.

The temptation to wear traditional clothing, stage rituals for photos, or perform in ways that "look" Celtic can be strong, especially online. It's normal to want to express belonging through appearance or art, but outward symbols without context risk flattening lived traditions into aesthetics. Instead, focus on gestures that feed genuine relationship—with landscape, seasons, ancestors, or community. Quiet persistence often has more heart than grand displays, reminding us that connection grows through consistency, not volume (Blackstock, 2024).

Attribution Habit: Credit Tradition-Bearers by Name and Place

Giving credit where it's due not only honors tradition but also threads you into the living story of knowledge-keeping. When sharing a charm, mention who preserved it and how it traveled to you. For instance: "This protection rhyme comes from Jennie McNeill, gathered by researcher Eilis O'Driscoll in Mayo, Ireland, 1952; I've adapted the wording slightly for clarity." If you post online, use captions or hashtags for quick attribution. Teaching a class or chatting with friends? A simple acknowledgment—"from a Shetland folktale retold by my great-uncle"—shows your respect.

Some worry that citing sources ruins the magic or interrupts the flow of conversation. In reality, even casual or brief attributions model respect and teach others to value origins. It takes only a moment and adds depth to what you share. Practicing regular attribution shifts the culture from secrecy or vague "authenticity" toward open recognition of those who have kept traditions alive (Blackstock, 2024).

Resisting Certification: No Need for Invented Titles

There's a real urge to prove belonging with titles: "ordained Druidess," "licensed Celtic practitioner," "keeper of the old ways." In many cases, these designations carry little weight outside certain circles and may even undermine trust if they are invented or unrecognized. True authority in folk traditions is built over years through relationships, accountability, and consistent contribution—none of which can be fast-tracked with certificates or dramatic claims.

When someone asks for proof of your qualifications, direct attention back to your sources, collaborators, and learning process: "Everything I know comes from this book collection and conversations with local historians; I'm happy to recommend resources." Remind yourself and others that being a careful, respectful learner is both honorable and honest.

These principles of transparency and attribution become concrete through intentional self-inquiry. Putting them into practice means tuning in to your own motives and habits—a process we'll explore next through guided reflection (Blackstock, 2024).

Reflective Integration

After exploring how to share and practice without overstepping, you're ready to turn that same ethical lens inward. Understanding boundaries with traditions and communities matters—but nothing shapes your engagement more than honest self-examination. You can't practice responsibly just by learning rules; you need tools that help you spot your own blind spots, desires, and the ripple effects of your actions.

Motivation Mapping: Why do you seek this knowledge?

Before reaching for any spell, story, or artifact, start by mapping your motivations. Make three lists: one called "Personal Healing," another "Cultural Heritage," and another "Academic Interest." Under each heading, write down three reasons that stir your curiosity. You might place "finding spiritual grounding" or "seeking connection after loss" in Personal Healing; "honoring grandmother's stories" or "reconnecting with ancestral lands" in Cultural Heritage; "understanding folklore preservation" or "studying regional variations" in Academic Interest. Take a moment to ask if unspoken motives—such as wanting status, belonging, or validation—are tucked somewhere deeper. Let yourself name these impulses without judgment; just seeing them helps you redirect energy toward humble learning instead of seeking authority.

Notice what emotions come up as you write. For example, nostalgia might pull you to see traditions through rose-tinted glasses, while validation-seeking could blur your ability to hear criticism from community members. Jot down two sentences about how each emotion could color your interpretation of stories, rituals, or roles. Returning to this exercise every few months will reveal patterns you might miss in the moment. Sometimes a longing for belonging draws you forward, other times excitement blindsides caution. Only regular check-ins will show you how motivation changes with experience (Winkelman et al., 1982).

Impact Forecast: Who benefits, who might be harmed?

When engaging with living traditions, consider not just your intentions but also the wider effects. Draw a diagram with yourself at the center. Around you, map out four rings: immediate community (family, local practitioners), regional communities (Irish, Scottish, Welsh, Breton culture-bearers), site caretakers (those tending land or sacred sites), and broader audiences (your followers, students, readers). For each, write two or three ways your participation might bring positive results—like helping preserve a song or raising awareness of an endangered custom—and two or three possible harms. For example, posting photos with exact GPS tags might mean your online friends discover a holy well, but sudden new visitors could damage it or disrupt local stewardship.

List scenarios that could arise from your sharing or teaching: Does describing a ritual misrepresent its living meaning? Could your enthusiasm make it harder for local voices to be heard? Add concrete mitigations beside each harm. These could include using general area names, adding background context, talking to local guides before publishing, or choosing silence when needed. Sometimes the most responsible act is not sharing everything you know, especially if it could put people or places at risk (Winkelman et al., 1982).

Action Boundaries: What will you not do, and why?

To ground ethical intent in practice, set clear red lines for yourself. Write three "I will not…" statements, explaining where you draw the line and why. For instance: "I will not post audio recordings of elders without their written consent and compensation," "I will not perform rituals at gravesites or active worship locations," "I will not geotag precise locations of holy wells or sensitive sites," "I will not use Celtic practices in paid sessions without proper study and connection," "I will not claim lineage I have not earned." Beneath each, add two or three sentences on your reasoning—this links your boundaries directly to potential harms and the protection of living communities.

Next, define clear stop conditions. Examples include: "If three community members raise questions, I pause and seek feedback," "If a source cannot be verified, I won't share it," or "If a site is getting crowded, I withdraw my promotion until it recovers." Finally, choose someone—a trusted friend, mentor, or peer group—to act as an accountability partner. Before sharing, teaching, or recording, run down a checklist: Have I confirmed sources? Sought consent? Added enough background? Am I honoring or extracting? Consider who truly gains from each action (Winkelman et al., 1982).

Ongoing Review: Set times to reassess commitments

Ethics don't stay fixed. To keep growing, book time once every quarter to revisit all these steps. Mark your calendar now for review days. In a simple journal, reflect on prompts like: What did I learn this season? Did I get new feedback? Where did my boundaries work, and where do they need tweaking? Note moments you succeeded, and places you feel uneasy. If you discover a beloved ritual actually came from a Victorian collector, revise your materials. If you uncover trauma connected to a practice, move more slowly and seek guidance.

Make space to record decisions—"chose not to post about a certain well, later learned locals were worried about overcrowding"—and notice emerging patterns. Invite and document feedback from those with lived experience, and update your boundaries as understanding deepens. This is not about never making mistakes—it's about showing up, listening, and adjusting as you grow. Responsible folk magic always asks, "What am I missing? Who else is affected? Am I willing to change?" (Winkelman et al., 1982).

Bringing It All Together

Throughout this chapter, we've explored why it's so important to honor the real diversity within Celtic traditions. Instead of lumping everything under one broad label, we've seen how each region—whether Irish, Scottish, Welsh, or Breton—carries its own language, customs, and stories. By taking the time to use specific place names, listen to local voices, and learn the meaning behind words and rituals, you start to move away from surface-level curiosity and into deeper connection. Respecting boundaries and understanding who holds knowledge helps keep both traditions and people safe, and grounds your practice in care rather than assumption.

This process asks for ongoing self-reflection, not just rule-following. Checking in with yourself about motivations, considering the impact of your actions, and giving clear credit are all part of an ethical approach. Small gestures—like choosing not to share certain details, seeking consent, or supporting living language efforts—make a difference in building trust and respect. As you continue your journey, remember that learning is always evolving, and honest humility matters more than any claim to expertise. True engagement means honoring both tradition and the communities who carry it forward—one thoughtful step at a time.

Chapter 10: Carrying the Flame: A Thoughtful Path Forward

Picture ten years from now a quiet coastal path in Brittany where the bracken stays neatly trimmed, not because of signs or rules, but because neighbors quietly tend it together. Imagine an Irish holy well still alive with fresh ribbons tied only by those who have always cared for it, their connections unbroken across time. Think about a community garden in Chicago that marks solstices with poems shared on benches, weather notes pinned to boards, and bread passed around as a simple celebration. These moments aren't grand or loud; they are gentle, woven into everyday life. The stories behind them are told with respect, elders are thanked for their wisdom, and new voices find a place—all blending to keep the spirit alive without turning these places into static exhibits.

What holds these scenes together isn't copying old customs exactly, but a living process of care that shifts with each season. This chapter opens a window to that future, inviting you to see legacy not as something locked away but as relationships growing through attention and kindness. It explores how traditions can thrive when nurtured thoughtfully—when people connect deeply to places and each other, choosing to carry a flame forward by making space for change, consent, and connection rather than simply repeating what came before.

A Living Legacy, Not a Museum

Traditions endure and grow through living relationship, not through being placed behind glass. Picking up litter by a neighborhood stream, or quietly tending a local hedgerow, can echo the reverence ancestors showed for sacred wells or boundary crossings. These gestures turn concern for heritage into daily care, letting each person nurture the relationship between people and place in ways that suit their lives (as described in Chapter 6). Letting tradition breathe means seeing it as an ongoing practice, shaped by attention and response. Building on the ethical boundaries we established earlier, care involves seeking permission, too—emailing a landowner before cleaning up a spring, or dropping a note to a park council about quiet stewardship plans. Actions rooted in consent and cooperation honor both community and land, shifting focus from imposing agendas to meeting actual needs (see Chapter 9).

Observing nature's small changes offers another point of connection. Watching for new leaves in spring, recording birdsong at dawn, or noting the flow of water after rain mirrors the seasonal noticing described in Chapter 4. These small acts create a tapestry of memory and belonging, growing understanding over time without pressure for perfection.

Chapter 10: Carrying the Flame: A Thoughtful Path Forward

Small observations gathered with regularity deepen insight, much like phenology practices where past generations learned local cycles by careful watching rather than formal ritual.

Simple rituals at home endure better than dramatic reenactments in borrowed landscapes. Lighting a candle near the kitchen sink on a festival night, or leaving clean water and bread on a windowsill, brings meaning close and keeps it manageable. The hearth practices outlined in Chapter 7 show how everyday acts carry memory forward. This approach keeps tradition from being frozen or made inaccessible. Instead, modest offerings—wildflowers gathered during a walk, or fresh herbs from a garden, always using what is abundant locally—offer care while supporting regenerative ethics highlighted in Chapters 5 and 8.

Practices thrive when paired to natural rhythms. Using monthly home altars or marking the start of each outdoor season welcomes the living world as companion, not backdrop. These moments feel gentle, guided by seasonal cues introduced in Chapter 4—the first frost, early dusk, fresh blossoms hinting at change. Seasonal companionship grows roots over years, teaching patience and humility. Winter months lend themselves to research and listening, spring invites planting and gentle maintenance, summer welcomes service outdoors, and autumn holds thankfulness and archiving. Patterns reflect cycles, not schedules, making space for adaptation and forgiveness.

Story stewardship asks for care as well. When retelling stories, protection charms, or experiences, crediting sources honors the living thread of community wisdom. Use citations or notes to make clear whether a charm comes from a Highland collection, a Breton family, or your own experience, just as the source citation practices in Chapter 9 encourage. Seek permission before describing stories still alive in a family or sharing images of fragile places, protecting privacy and relationship as discussed in Chapter 3 and Chapter 6. Keeping notes on local versions lets differences flourish instead of pressing for a single correct way, guarding against the flattening effect of homogenization mentioned in Chapter 9.

Care extends across distance. For those far from ancestral lands, tending a city tree, keeping a record of backyard birds, or creating rituals suited to the present place cultivates connection. It's not distance that erases belonging, but neglect. Honoring legacy doesn't demand grand gestures or perfect knowledge; it grows from steady, heartfelt effort. Each small act—lighting a candle, picking up trash, thanking a neighbor who shares a story—carries the flame forward, ensuring Celtic folk magic remains a living, breathing legacy.

Diaspora and Homecoming

The living legacy we've just explored takes on special complexity for those whose ancestors came from Celtic lands, yet whose lives unfold far away. This tug between heritage and place is real—and you are not alone in feeling it. So many carry the stories, songs, or surnames of Ireland, Scotland, Wales, Cornwall, or Brittany, but wake each morning to city skylines,

Chapter 10: Carrying the Flame: A Thoughtful Path Forward

prairie winds, or desert sun. Longing for connection—to language, landscape, rituals—can show up as ache, confusion, hope, or guilt. Each emotion deserves space. The pull is not an error. It marks your care.

You never have to flatten these two places into one box. Loving both the land of your ancestors and the land beneath your feet is possible. Instead of blending traditions into something generic, try holding separate observances that honor each distinctly. Maybe you light a candle at Imbolc for Brigid, reading aloud about her wells in Kildare, while a week later you volunteer at your local river's cleanup. Start a practice of alternating: Irish roots one month, Scottish the next, or even bringing non-Celtic lineages into their own time. You can split your donations too—supporting a conservation project near your family's origin, and also giving to efforts in your current home. Each act says: I see you, I care for you, even if I am far (Ó Giolláin, 2000).

Remember our earlier exploration of naming regions specifically—this practice becomes vital when distance tempts you to romanticize or flatten traditions. Naming keeps memory honest. Consent and permission protocols matter doubly when you're a guest in ancestral lands or visiting sacred sites online. Refusing to blur boundaries honors both your origins and where you live now (Harvey, 2019).

Knowledge keepers rooted in place—elders, historians, folklorists, and teachers living in these lands—hold the threads you seek. Lean toward learning in context. If you visit Ireland, attend a guided walk led by a local historian or a small folklore workshop instead of relying only on books or internet lists.

Pay fairly for their work. Always check for community guidelines, and ask which stories are fine to share and which stay private. Sometimes you may be told "no photos" or "not here"—that's a form of care, not exclusion. When you go home, bring the same mindset to your current region: look for talks by indigenous educators or park rangers, find out how local stories are told, honor permissions given, and support with time, money, or advocacy (MacEachen, 2021).

Heritage travel or pilgrimage can feel like coming home, but tread gently. Move quietly, in small groups or alone, sticking to marked paths and respecting fragile land. Try to travel off-peak, reducing pressure on popular sites. Bring nothing away except memories, and leave nothing behind except thanks—no ribbons, no rocks, only a donation to site caretakers if you wish. Learning a few basic phrases in Irish, Scottish Gaelic, Welsh, or Breton shows respect, even if you only use them to read plaques or say "hello." And if you're unsure what is welcome at a holy well or grave, choose silence and gratitude over leaving objects. Presence, listening, and real support count more than performance or proof (Ó Giolláin, 2000; McNeill, 1956).

Translating values means rooting yourself where you actually live. Adopting a tree, river, or park nearby as your seasonal anchor builds the kind of relationship old Celtic communities had with local groves and wells. Attend to the rhythms of your weather and land—watch spring arrive, notice autumn's shift, learn which native plants feed birds or pollinators and which festivals already shape neighborhood life. If you harvest, do so legally, respectfully, giving back as much as you take. Dig into the indigenous and settler histories of your region, and lift up community projects rather than importing rituals wholesale. For example, collect leaves during the equinox in the Pacific Northwest and observe salmon runs, letting the place teach you. Practice grounded symbolism instead of layering borrowed meaning onto unfamiliar earth (Harvey, 2019).

You might wonder if being a "real" Celtic practitioner means living only in ancestral places or knowing every custom. The answer is no. True devotion grows where care and accountability meet. Mixed identities enrich the story—hold Irish and African American, Scottish and Filipino, or any blend without shrinking either part. Hold yourself gently if grief for lost language or unknown ancestors stings. Every thoughtful step you take—toward research, generosity, local engagement—lights a way forward, honoring both home and homeland.

Designing Personal Reflection Cycles

After so much learning—about regional traditions, ethical boundaries, and cycles of nature—it's common to feel both inspired and a bit uncertain where to begin. You might wonder how all these ideas connect in your day-to-day life, or worry about keeping up with every season and custom. A flexible reflection cycle can ease this pressure. It offers a gentle frame that supports growth year after year, adapting as your relationship with place and ancestry shifts. What matters most is the act of returning, not getting everything perfect from the start.

You're invited to try a hands-on journaling exercise as you read. Grab your favorite notebook or open a blank digital document. This practice helps shape a seasonal plan that honors both your heritage and the ecosystem around you. The goal isn't to copy ancient rituals exactly. Instead, you'll build something alive that suits today's world and respects living traditions (see Chapter 9 for more on cultural sensitivity). Allow yourself 30–45 minutes for this first outline. Let it be nourishing—a source of rest, not another obligation. Remember, you can revisit and reshape your cycle any time you wish.

Step 1: Choose Four Markers

Begin by picking four dates or events that naturally divide your year into quarters. In some places, traditional Celtic markers like solstices, equinoxes, or Imbolc and Samhain match well with natural changes—if that speaks to you, start there. But in other climates, these dates might not line up with visible shifts. Instead, look for markers like the arrival of monsoon rains, the first frost, salmon runs, or a local festival in your town. Each marker should mean something: maybe the spring equinox reminds you of family stories passed down from Irish grandparents, or maybe a local autumn harvest pairs with memories of feasting. Write each selected marker along with a sentence or two about why it matters to you. Is it linked to ecology, a personal milestone, or ancestral tradition? Mix and match as needed. For each marker, decide how much time you can realistically spend—30 to 60 minutes is enough for most folks. If fitting four feels too much, start with two and see how it goes; there's room to expand later.

Step 2: Set Listening Practices

Now, choose simple practices for each marker that help you notice change and deepen connection. For each date, design a three-part check-in. First: take a mindful walk, free from phones or podcasts. Pay attention to plants, animals, weather, people—write down three things that have changed since your last marker. Maybe "Spring: wild violets blooming, ducks returning, neighbors cleaning yards." Second: pair your walk with a short reading. It could be a folktale from Scotland, a poem from a local writer, or an article about seasonal customs in your area. Third: observe the sky—where is the sun setting or rising, are clouds different, does the moon stand out tonight? These practices are easy to adapt whether you're city-based or rural, energetic or limited by mobility. Aim for no more than an hour total per marker. If a walk is hard, sitting by a window with tea works well. The point isn't perfection, but showing up. If you miss a season, jot down why and what might help next time (drawing on Chapter 4's guidance about seasonal awareness).

Step 3: Document with Care

Create a one-page template for recording each seasonal check-in. Include the date and general place ("city park" or "my balcony," never geotags), weather, three observations from your walk, what you read and the reason for that choice, plus sky notes. Add a short space for feelings or insights—did a memory surface? Did you learn a new story from a friend or neighbor? Whenever you include folk wisdom, history, or community knowledge, cite where it came from: list the book, museum, or conversation partner's name (and get permission if sharing publicly). Finish each page by answering: "What is this season teaching me right now?" This habit not only deepens your self-awareness, it also protects landscapes (no secret sites broadcasted) and communities (attributing knowledge and honoring consent). Such careful documentation reflects the ethics developed in Chapter 9.

Step 4: Quarterly Review

At the end of each quarter—right before beginning the new marker—pause for a quick review in your journal. Ask yourself: Which practices felt nourishing? Were any steps draining or stressful? Did you notice impact on the local environment, good or bad? Did your presence support, disturb, or leave no trace? Consider whether anything risked crossing boundaries, like overcrowding a beloved park or using closed cultural material. Jot down a goal for the next quarter: maybe learning a word in Welsh, tending a native plant, or sharing a home-cooked meal. See this as gentle adjustment, not critique. Changes show responsiveness and respect for both your needs and the larger web of relationship (recalling stewardship themes from earlier chapters).

Trying something new brings its own kind of vulnerability, especially when it matters to your sense of belonging. Remember: the point isn't to do everything flawlessly, but to show up with care and honesty. Start small, even if just tracking two markers for now. Over time, these personal cycles become steady ways to carry the flame of tradition—quietly, consistently, with real roots. This practice lays the path for longer-term commitment, which takes shape in the next part of your journey.

The Quiet Commitment

Now that you've established your rhythm through the seasons—with four markers, listening practices, and regular reviews—the question becomes how this work can shape a life instead of just a year. The small habits you built are seeds for something much longer: sustained care that rarely trends or attracts attention but always grows roots. Your documentation, careful listening, and seasonal markers are only the beginning. They guide you toward a path where intention outlasts novelty—where practice slips quietly into daily life and ripples outward over years.

Patience is the first gift you'll need to nurture as you move from cycles to legacy. In a world where social media celebrates spectacle and quick transformation, slow learning may feel nearly invisible. Yet, the quiet act of returning to the same story circle each autumn, greeting elders at local heritage talks, or adding a phrase or two to your Irish vocabulary over a whole year weaves true intimacy with tradition that fast consumption cannot match. Choosing to visit one holy well in every season—watching water levels change, tracking plant growth, noticing offerings left by neighbors—teaches more than racing to collect photos of twenty sites. Writing a private letter to yourself each winter, or checking in with a trusted friend about your journey, offers honest milestones. Public displays often fracture what could become an accountable relationship between you and place; restraint in sharing keeps some commitments sacred, grounded, and tied to real land and people (see Chapter 9).

Throughout this book, we've seen that lasting folk magic is rooted not in performance but in reciprocity and service. The chapter on household customs showed that humble acts—lighting a candle, tending a hearth—carry legacy because they are repeated, ordinary, and shared (Chapter 7). These values stretch outdoors too. Bringing a pair of gloves and a trash bag on every walk means you clean up paths near ancient stones as a silent offering. Giving a few hours to help at a conservation day, or sending a monthly donation to a regional archive, ensures the physical and cultural landscape remains healthy. You might keep a modest kit in your car: gloves, sturdy boots, notebook, small envelopes for respectfully collecting a fallen leaf or pebble. When you tidy a trail, tend a well, or jot down changes in plant growth, you enact stewardship that is both practical and magical. Small acts repeated often become the fabric that holds living traditions together (Chapters 3 & 7).

Learning companions gather along the way, both in human form and as tools. A steady reading habit—rotating between folklore anthologies, regional ecology, and contemporary voices—keeps curiosity alive without burnout. Revisiting your most cherished stories once a year lets new insights emerge as your experience matures. Language learning can be gentle: five phrases learned slowly, written in your field notes, practiced aloud during walks, used to greet a neighbor or interpret place names on old maps. Weather logs, sketches of seasonal plants, or a timeline of visits to a single site gradually fill your notebook with depth. These records will someday tell a story across decades, showing how your understanding of places, languages, and customs has grown much like the land itself—layer upon layer, year upon year.

Returning to the principles explored in earlier chapters, ethical legacy grows from respect for boundaries, community voices, and transparency. As you document sites, always record who taught you the lore, whether you have permission to share, and any requests made by caretakers (Chapter 9). When someone new asks for guidance, offer introductions—to local experts, to elders, to those whose lived experience anchors wisdom. Share your process honestly: describe your own mistakes and long detours as evidence that everyone starts somewhere, and patience is part of the path. Consider how you might support language classes or conservation projects not just now, but far beyond your lifetime—by naming heritage nonprofits, archives, or ecological funds in your will. Picture future learners finding clear notes with sources cited, permissions listed, and context explained, so nobody must dig through confusion. This is how intention becomes legacy: you received gifts of place, story, and care; your choices preserve and enrich these gifts for everyone who follows.

Picture yourself ten years from now, still tending the same well, reading new footnotes beside your old field sketches, guiding a newcomer past blackberry brambles to the stone that first called you here. Choose one small action from your quarterly plan to carry forward—tidy a path, write a letter, learn a phrase. Let these be enough. Quiet commitment, kept close and lived fully, is the strongest anchor you can give to Celtic folk magic.

Final Thoughts

Looking ahead, it becomes clear that what lasts is not the rigid copying of rituals or the preservation of fixed gestures. Instead, legacy thrives when we nurture relationships—with land, ancestors, neighbors, and new voices—through simple, ongoing acts of care. Whether it's trimming bracken on a familiar path, tying ribbons at a well, or celebrating the solstice with friends in a city garden, these gentle habits let tradition remain alive, porous, and welcoming. The stories and practices you choose to carry forward matter because they are shaped by your love and presence, not because they are perfect replicas of the past.

Letting tradition breathe means honoring where it came from, giving credit to those who nurtured it before you, and opening space for new participation. You don't need grand gestures to keep this living fabric strong; small steady actions and thoughtful stewardship make the difference. Through ongoing attention, honest reflection, and respect for both roots and evolving rhythms, you help weave a future where heritage feels like home—real, changing, and full of possibility.

Conclusion

As you reach the close of this journey, I want to circle back to the heart of what we've explored together: Celtic folk magic is not a locked, ancient formula or a distant fantasy. Instead, it's a living tradition—woven into daily routines, rooted in kinship with land and people, and alive in every act of tending, blessing, and remembering. This book's core hope was to shine a light on how these traditions are gentle flames passed hand to hand—not static rules or relics. By reading, questioning, and reflecting, you've stepped into that same current, learning how ancestral wisdom and present-day experience can meet in meaningful, everyday moments.

Throughout these pages, we've celebrated the beautiful complexity found in Irish, Scottish, Welsh, and Breton customs. Each region offers its own languages, stories, plants, songs, and ways of marking time. There isn't one single "Celtic" way—there are dozens, each shaped by place, history, and living memory. Authenticity comes from meeting each tradition on its own terms, paying attention to local details, community voices, and the rhythms of the land. When you see the diversity—not as confusion or contradiction, but as creative strength—you recognize that every charm, festival, or household gesture gains its meaning from context, relationship, and story.

One of the most important lessons we've returned to again and again is the deep need for ethical reflection and responsible engagement. Whether you're inspired to make a Brigid's cross, visit a holy well, or share a blessing with friends, intention only matters when matched by respect for the people and places behind the tradition. Consent, humility, and attribution aren't just ideal—they are vital. They guard against appropriation, avoid turning living heritage into an aesthetic or commodity, and ensure that your practices support rather than erase those whose ancestors carried this wisdom through hardship and change. When you choose modest, local actions—tending a tree, learning a word in Gaelic, supporting a craftsperson—you're acting not out of nostalgia, but out of relationship and care.

Every reader who completes this book deserves acknowledgement for showing up with curiosity, openness, and a willingness to go deeper than surface-level images and quick-fix spells. You've walked through the tangled histories of language, faith, and survival; you've listened to layered stories about saints, wells, weather, and boundaries. You've learned to spot differences between Victorian invention and local memory, and to see value in questions and honest uncertainty. That commitment—to moving slowly, honoring gaps in knowledge, and letting lived experience shape understanding—marks the real transition from outsider curiosity to respectful, informed engagement. Wherever you started, you now have the tools and discernment to navigate folklore, spirituality, and heritage in a truthful, caring way.

Yet finishing a book is never the end; it's only the turning of another year on the wheel. I invite you to continue building connection through steady, simple practices. Keep a journal of seasonal changes where you live, follow the arrival of birds or the blooming of local flowers, pay attention to the rituals that emerge naturally around food, light, and thresholds in your home. Let small acts—lighting a candle at dusk, offering gratitude before a meal, walking familiar paths at dawn—anchor you in the cycles that shaped so much of the folk magic we've explored. These observations not only deepen your personal sense of belonging, but tie you into the same attentive presence that guided countless generations before you.

Connection doesn't thrive in isolation. Sharing stories, questions, and discoveries with friends—online or face-to-face—keeps tradition dynamic and relevant. If you feel moved, join local groups invested in folk heritage, language revival, native plant stewardship, or cultural festivals. Support storytellers, musicians, historians, artists, and elders who keep wisdom alive, whether by listening, volunteering, or donating. Share what you learn, always giving credit, and stay open to being corrected or guided by those who hold deeper roots. In helping tend both the wild lands outside and the invisible threads of story inside, you become part of the community of caretakers keeping these traditions vibrant and evolving.

Through all of this, please know how grateful I am for your trust, attention, and willingness to explore with nuance and compassion. Your effort helps shape the future of Celtic folkways, not by preserving them unchanged, but by carrying their spirit forward in new and thoughtful ways. You are invited, now and always, to see yourself as a steward—someone who listens deeply, acts with gentle hands, honors permission and story, and finds joy in mutual care. Together, we can keep weaving a living legacy that sustains not just memory, but possibility—so that the magic of belonging, reciprocity, and respect stays bright in our homes, communities, and hearts.

Reference List

(2025). Studyguides.com. https://studyguides.com/study-methods/study-guide/cmiw85jy463eo01aauultlkbo

A Pagan's Perspective: Critiques of Christianity. (2024). Lemon8. https://www.lemon8-app.com/@lunrluvrrr/7366655944484258309?region=us

Banda, C. V., Banda, J. T., & Singini, T. (2024, September 1). *Preserving Cultural Heritage: A Community-Centric Approach to Safeguarding the Khulubvi Traditional Temple Malawi.* Heliyon; Elsevier BV. https://doi.org/10.1016/j.heliyon.2024.e37610

Burnett, D. G. (2000, August 22). *Spiritual Conflict and Folk Religion.* Lausanne Movement. https://lausanne.org/content/folk-religion

Blackstock, J. (2024, April 14). *Paganism: Insights from Anthropology, Psychology, and Comparative Religion.* Taproot Therapy Collective. https://gettherapybirmingham.com/the-true-nature-of-paganism-insights-from-anthropology-psychology-and-comparative-religion/

Borkowicz, P. (2025). *G. Gary - Wisht Waters - The Cult and Magic of Water.* Scribd. https://www.scribd.com/

document/887535945/G-Gary-Wisht-Waters-The-Cult-and-Magic-of-Water

Campbell, M. (2025, July 24). *92. Sacred Places, Sacred Latitudes*. Mounds, Hills and Mo. https://www.mercurialpathways.com/post/92-sacred-places-sacred-latitudes

Electric Witch. (2025, December 9). *Rowan Trees by the Door: Old European Folklore*. Wild Witch Herbs. https://wildwitchherbs.com/rowan-trees-front-door-old-world-folklore/

Gebhardt, M. (2024, February 6). *Weather forecast with animals, plants or clouds - assessing the weather through observation of nature*. Survival Kompass. https://survival-kompass.de/en/weather-forecast-through-nature-observations/

Grokipedia. (1970, January 21). *History of the Irish language*. Grokipedia. https://grokipedia.com/page/History_of_the_Irish_language

Llygedyn Grove. (2025). Llygedyngrove.org. http://llygedyngrove.org/Ethics.htm

Long, P. R., Petrokofsky, L., Harvey, W. J., Orsi, P., Jordon, M. W., & Petrokofsky, G. (2025, August 1). *Structural Diversity and Biodiversity of Forest and Hedgerow in Areas Managed for Pheasant Shooting Across the UK*. Forests. https://doi.org/10.3390/f16081249

The CR FAQ - An Introduction to Celtic Reconstructionist Paganism - Intermediate Questions. (2025). Paganachd.com. https://www.paganachd.com/faq/intermediate.html

The Guardian Trees of Ireland | Irish folkore from the Emerald Isle. (n.d.). Emeraldisle.ie. https://emeraldisle.ie/the-guardian-trees-of-ireland

UNESCO. (2019). *Oral traditions and expressions including language as a vehicle of the intangible cultural heritage.* Unesco. https://ich.unesco.org/en/oral-traditions-and-expressions-00053

VAI_Projects. (2025, July 14). *Undertaking Commissions.* Visual Artists Ireland. https://visualartists.ie/how-to-manual/undertaking-commissions

Venutius. (2024, July 7). *Early Christian syncretism and how the old ones hid amongst the new religion.* Brigantes Nation. https://brigantesnation.com/early-christian-syncretism-and-how-the-old-ones-hid-amongst-the-new-religion/

Winkelman, M., Ankenbrandt, K. W., Bharati, A., Bourguignon, E., Dobkin, M., Dundes, A., Eisenbud, J., Goodman, F. D., Hallpike, C. R., Hultkrantz, A., Åke Hultkrantz, Jarvie, I. C., Lex, B. W., Long, J. K., Moss, L. W., Preston, R. J., RomanucciRoss, L., Sebald, H., Sheils, D., & Singer, P. (1982). *Magic: A Theoretical Reassessment [and Comments and Replies].* Current Anthropology; [The University of Chicago Press, WennerGren Foundation for Anthropological Research]; JSTOR. https://doi.org/10.2307/2742551

Reference List

Word Filter. (2025). Pakin.org. https://www.pakin.org/wordfilter

aihowells. (2025). *A Social History of Ancient Ireland 1*. Scribd. https://www.scribd.com/document/110685116/A-Social-History-of-Ancient-Ireland-1

ipsadmin. (2024, July 5). *Irish Pagan Holidays - The Irish Pagan School*. The Irish Pagan School. https://irishpagan.school/irish-pagan-holidays/

lovedoesthat. (2024, October 15). *3 Key Lessons for Journaling in Difficult Seasons - Love Does That | Kari Bartkus*. Love Does That | Kari Bartkus - Author and Speaker. https://lovedoesthat.org/3-key-lessons-for-journaling-in-difficult-seasons/

www.ingramcontent.com/pod-product-compliance
Lightning Source LLC
Chambersburg PA
CBHW050637160426
43194CB00010B/1706